Compact Guide: Crete is the ideal quick-reference guide to this island of Zorba and Zeus. It tells you everything you need to know about Crete's many attractions, from bustling ports to remote mountain villages, gorgeous beaches to dramatic gorges, and lively tavernas to lost civilisations.

This is just one title in *Apa Publications'* new series of pocket-sized, easy-to-use guidebooks intended for the independent-minded traveller. Based on an award-winning formula pioneered in Germany, *Compact Guides* pride themselves on being up-to-date and authoritative. They are in essence mini travel encyclopedias, designed to be comprehensive yet portable, both readable and reliable.

Star Attractions

An instant reference to some of Crete's most popular tourist attractions to help you on your way.

Palace of Knossos p20

Zaros p27

Snake Goddess p15

Minoan Palace of Agia Triada p31

Arkadi Monastery p34

Lassithi p40

Gournia p46

Rethymnon p50

Chania's Venetian harbour p58

Samaria Gorge p62

Elafonisi p67

CReTe

Introduction

Places

Culture

Leisure

Practical Information

Crete – Holiday Island and Cradle of Europe

Crete always makes a perfect holiday destination. This varied island has something to offer everyone. Watersport enthusiasts will find the cleanest water in Greece. Walkers will find a network of old bridlepaths as well as many waymarked tracks winding through lonely villages, idyllic landscapes and impressive gorges. For those who just want to enjoy the sun and soak up the atmosphere, Crete enjoys 300 days of sun per year and can offer quiet, isolated coves and big, crowded beaches, small resorts and major centres. Everyone, whether they are in search of peace and quiet or a range of new and exciting experiences, will find something to suit them on Crete.

A familiar sound

The Greek epic poet Homer in the 8th century BC described Crete as a 'fair and fertile land in the midst of a wine-dark sea washed by waves on every side'. Two thousand years earlier the southernmost Mediterranean island had seen the emergence of Europe's first advanced civilisation. The frescoes at Knossos paint a picture of a world at peace, a world with a love of life, of sport and games. Minoan artists chose not to portray their rulers, preferring splendidly clothed or bare-breasted women. According to Homer, King Minos controlled Knossos and the labyrinth. His daughter Ariadne gave Theseus, her lover, a ball of thread so that he could find his way out of the maze after he had killed the Minotaur, the half-bull, half-man monster. For the Greeks who later settled on Crete, Minoan culture was so important that they adopted the Cretan myth of Zeus, the father of both gods and men, being brought up in the Cretan caves. In later life Zeus turned into a bull and carried off a Phoenician king's daughter by the name of Europa, who later lent her name to the continent. A visit to Knossos and the archaeological museum in Heraklion with its unique record of Minoan civilisation should be included in every holidaymaker's itinerary, for the earliest traces of European civilisation lie in the history of Crete and Greek mythology.

5

Women of Knossos

Position and Landscape

Crete, Greece's southernmost island, lies between Europe, Asia and Africa. The offshore island of Gavdos is the southernmost point in Europe. With a length of 257km (159 miles) the island is big enough and varied enough to accommodate its visitors without them treading on each other's toes. Surface area excluding the nearby islands is 8,259sq km (3,138sq miles), just under two and a half times that of Majorca and about half that of Hawaii. At its narrowest

point near Ierapetra, the island is only 12km (7 miles) wide, while near Heraklion, the island's administrative centre, 62km (38 miles) separate the north and south coast.

Mountains which remain snow-capped until June dominate the Cretan landscape. The island is broken up into four ranges. Furthest west are the White Mountains or Lefka Ori (2,452m/8,042ft), in the centre stands the Ida Range with the island's highest mountain, Psiloritis (2,456m/8,055ft), and in the east the Lassithi Range whose highest point is Mount Dikte at 2,148m (7,045ft). In the far west are the Sitia Mountains (1,450m/4,756ft). The predominantly limestone mountains emerged during the Tertiary Era with Crete a part of the Dinaric-Taurus range (Balkan peninsula and Taurus mountains). The southern coast of Crete lies on the line between the Eurasian and African plates – the cause of several earthquakes which have struck the island in recorded time. The mountains on the south side of the island, therefore, drop steeply into the sea, while in the north, they slope gently down through coastal plains to the water. Distinctive geological features include over 3,000 grottoes, wild, often inaccessible gorges and broad, fertile plains.

6

Climate

Crete is an island for every season. In the summer the *meltimi*, a fresh, northerly wind, helps to moderate temperatures, while in the winter the south coast with its palm trees and bananas is always pleasant. Mountain climbers should wait until June when the peaks are free of snow. For a botanist and also the devotee of art and culture, spring and autumn are the best times of year to visit. In the winter months and often well into April it can be quite chilly on the north coast. Small hotels and rooms have no heating, so travellers are advised to take a warm sleeping bag or a hot-water bottle. A torch is useful in caves and for illuminating the gloomy corners of Byzantine churches. Bathing shoes will help to protect feet from sharp-edged rocks on the beaches.

Nature and the Environment

The Samaria Gorge

The island's once rich woodland has been destroyed to make way for the olive trees which are thought to number over 25 million. Not all of them are harvested as the price of olive oil has fallen sharply. Carob or St John's Bread and chestnuts are cultivated mainly in the west, while cypresses, chestnut oaks and planes proliferate in the narrow gorges of the south coast. The undisputed natural highlight of Crete is the Samaria Gorge, one of the deepest gorges in Europe. As well as being the last natural habitat of the threatened Cretan wild goat (also known as the kri kri), the gorge is home to a variety of orchid,

There is an interesting selection of wild herbs. *Dictamos* (or dittany) was exported in ancient times as it was said to stem the flow of blood from a wound. Other prized qualities were as an aphrodisiac and as a treatment for gall bladder complaints.

Wild herbs

Crete has no heavy industry, so is generally pollution-free, apart from in the towns where exhaust fumes can be slow to disperse. All towns are now equipped with sewage treatment plants, most of the funds having come from a major European Union programme to clean up the Mediterranean. Crete's first wind farm near Toplou aims to harness natural energy, but solar energy has been in use for many years. Many houses have a solar panel to supply warm water.

The Greeks have become heavily dependent on plastic – not only for mineral water and shopping bags, but also to cover greenhouses. A major environmental problem has arisen in Crete as these plastic sheets tear and blow off in the winter storms and little is done to clear up the waste. The issue of waste disposal is being addressed by the Greek government, but the day when local authorities stop burning rubbish is still some way off. Tourists are inclined to buy bottled water, but in Cretan villages, fresh, untreated spring water gushes from the taps. Only in the cities is the water lightly chlorinated.

Population

Cretans have shaped 8,000 years of history, but they have only rarely had a free hand in shaping their own destiny. In 67BC Crete became a part of the Roman empire and with the island occupying a position of such strategic importance, it is no surprise that independence did not return until 1898. The occupying forces – Romans, Arabs, Venetians and Turks, and more recently the Germans – were never able to force the native people into submission. On the contrary, resistance lasting centuries has shaped the character of the islanders. It manifests itself now in a type of authoritarianism, pride, a mistrust of the 'government' from Athens and a highly developed sense of honour or *philotimo*. If honour was impugned, revenge, even in recent times, was demanded. The Cretan costume is an expression of a past, fashioned by the resistance struggle: black out of respect for lost relatives and 'for Crete', polished military-style boots and a dagger tucked in the belt. Another long-established custom – and one which obviously stems from less peaceful times – is for every Cretan man to carry a firearm.

Proud to be Cretan

Family photographs in *kafenia* and *tavernas* invariably show the proud head of the family posing with a weapon in his hand and an ammunition belt across his torso. Road signs riddled with bullet holes will have been used for tar-

Many hands make light work

get practice. Salvoes fired into the air at village weddings pay tribute to the newly-weds.

Cretans can often be identified by their names, with '-akis' as a typical ending. This suffix means 'son of', so Theodorakis means 'Theodor junior'.

Customs and Festivals

Farmers start early

The lives of the Cretans are regulated by a daily and yearly rhythm. Farmers start their work very early. Breakfast or *kolatsio* of olives, cheese and bread follows after a few hours. At home, they may drink a warm milky soup and perhaps dip their bread or dark rusks into it. They only retire to the *kafenion* when it gets too hot to work.

In the towns, many manual workers start the day with *patsas*, a hot, enriching soup made from cows' stomach. In the evenings Greek men gather in the *kafenion*. A young apprentice has to find his own *kafenion*. His own flat or that of his parents seems 'like a prison', as he puts it. Friends, acquaintances and business partners meet in the *kafenion*. Deals are struck there – often with a handshake, a binding agreement with the same effect as a signature. Women are not allowed in the *kafenion*.

Religious, national, cultural and family celebrations follow on from each other in a regular sequence *(see page 77)*. Baptisms, engagements, marriages and funerals, celebrations of saints' days, religious festivals or chestnut, snail, orange, wine and fishing festivals are all good opportunities to eat, drink and dance, with some celebrations lasting for days. Nearly all observant Cretans follow the Greek Orthodox religion.

Economy

The main elements of the Cretan economy are tourism and agriculture. Out of a population of about 600,000 and a working population of about 200,000 (including the self-employed and their dependents), some 100,000 work on the land. This statistic should be treated with caution as many manual workers give 'farmer' as their occupation to reduce tax.

In summer owners may let rooms in their houses. There are thought to be a total of about 150,000 beds to let on the island and the Greek Tourist Organisation estimates that between three and five people depend on the income from each bed and the related business. The population swells during the summer with seasonal workers converging on the island from all over Greece. Nevertheless, wages in Crete are about 35 percent of the average for the EU.

Cretan agriculture can be divided into two branches: traditional products such as olives, wine, sheep and goats, yoghurt, honey and cheese on the one hand and the more profitable greenhouse vegetables on the other. Since Greece joined the EU in 1981 the agribusinesses of the developed EU countries have competed fiercely with the Greek farmers. 'Greek feta cheese', for example, is often produced in Denmark, Holland or Germany and works out markedly cheaper than the genuine product. Prices of Cretan olive oil, reckoned by many to be the best in Europe, have dropped as a result of competition from 'Euro' olive oil. Only Cretan greenhouse vegetables have sold well at good prices, and not just in Greece but in supermarkets throughout the EU.

Succulent apricots

Cretan olives make excellent oil

Administration and Social Policy

Crete is one of Greece's thirteen provinces. The provinces are broken down into regional councils *(nomos,* plural *nomoi)* – there are four in Crete – and each one of these is made up of a number of districts *(eparchia, -ies).* The lowest levels of administration are the towns *(dimos, dimi)* and the parishes *(kinotita -tes).* The main policy decisions are made in Athens – Greece is run along highly centralised lines, particularly in relation to the 'national quota'. The state has about a 50 percent interest in all economic matters and takes a 70 percent stake in banks. The socialist PASOK which has been in power since October 1993 seeks to run all government concerns along political lines. Artificial jobs are created and firms facing bankruptcy are taken over by the state to save the jobs. Inflation is usually about the highest of all the EU countries.

The role of women in Greece was affected by legislation in 1983. Women were given equal status, the right of a man to receive a dowry from his future wife's parents as 'compensation' was abolished, civil marriages were permitted and divorce made a little easier. But long-standing traditions cannot easily be abandoned and change is slow to take place.

Venizelos, the man who united Crete and Greece

Historical Highlights

6500–3000BC Crete is settled by Anatolians during the Neolithic period. Hunters and gatherers establish permanent settlements and farm the land chiefly on the Messara plain. By the end of the Neolithic, copper tools are used widely.

3000–2200BC New settlers from lands further east bring further knowledge of metalworking with them. A Bronze Age culture emerges and is well established by the middle of the 3rd millenium. The Cretans bury their dead in communal tombs.

Early Palatial Period (2000–1700BC)

Minoan 'palaces' are built in Phaistos, Knossos, Malia and Kato Zakros around 2000BC. Archaeologists have not yet determined the social conditions which led to their construction.

Late Palatial Period (1700–1450BC)

The early 'palaces' fall victim to some natural catastrophe or military influence and new palaces are constructed on the ruins. With their main base at Knossos, the Minoans are now undisputedly the greatest maritime and trading power in the eastern Mediterranean. Skilled craftsmen, notably sculptors, potters, and metalworkers, bring great prosperity to the island. Local fresco painting is also developed into a fine art.

Mycenaean Period (1450–1150BC)

Crete is conquered by Mycenean troops from the Peloponnese. The palaces are destroyed. Only Knossos and Archanes are rebuilt and used by Myceneans, as indicated by weapons found at burial sites.

Greek City-States (about 1150–67BC)

The power of the Mycenean empire declines for reasons unknown. After 1200BC, Dorian Greeks overrun the island but bitter internal disputes are not resolved.

Hellenistic Period (from 330BC)

The city-states largely retain their independence from the nation states. Cretans serve as pirates or mercenaries for the major powers.

Roman Period

67BC Crete becomes a Roman province under Metallus 'Creticus'. Gortyn is made the capital of an area that encompasses Cyrenaica (now Libya) in north Africa.

59AD The apostle Paul lands at Kali Limenes on his way to Rome. His companion Titus remains on Crete to spread the word. The arrival of Christianity has a considerable impact, but only after Rome recognises Christianity in the 4th century and bans heathen sects in 391.

Byzantine Crete and the Arabs

395AD With the partition of the Roman Empire, Crete becomes part of the Eastern Empire with Constantinople (Byzantium) as its capital. The Byzantine State is characterised by the unity of church and state or Caesaropapism.

726–80 and **815–43** Iconoclastic doctrine rejects the worship of icons. Monasteries and churches are destroyed. Their wealth and property are confiscated.

826–961 Arabic occupation of Crete. The Arabs continue with the wholesale destruction of early Christian art and architecture. Heraklion is fortified and renamed Rabd el Kandak (the moat). The Venetians later corrupt the Arabic name to 'Candia' which describes the town and the whole island.

From 961 Nikiphorus Phokas recaptures Crete for the Byzantines. Economic fortunes improve under a military administration and churches and monasteries are founded. Sea trade is in the hands of the Genoese.

Venetian Domination

1204 Crusaders from the Fourth Crusade conquer the Christian-Orthodox Empire of Byzantium. Byzantine territory on Greek soil is divided up among Catholic feudal landowners. Crete is ruled from Venice which provided logistical support for the Crusaders and, having expelled the Genoese, now controls trade in the entire eastern Mediterranean. Rebellions fomented by Cretan landowners and their vassals shake their Venetian masters.

1453 Constantinople is defeated by the Turks. Greek intellectuals and artists seek refuge in Crete and initiate the 'Cretan Renaissance'.

16th and 17th centuries Venetian influence wanes and the Ottomans block overland trade with the Far East. Spain and Portugal discover alternative trade routes, with the result that the eastern Mediterranean ceases to be such an important commercial base.

Turkish Domination

1645 An invading force of 100,000 Ottoman soldiers lands at Chania. After 21 years of siege Heraklion falls to the occupying forces. About 30,000 Venetians and allied forces oppose Turkish rule, but the Turks dispossess Venetian landowners, giving the land back to the Cretans. Many native Turks settle on the island.

1770–1 During the Russo-Turkish War of 1768–74 many Greek territories rebel against Turkish rule. Greeks ally with their Russian Orthodox brothers. The uprising in Crete centres on the Sfakia Mountains. When the rebellion fails, the leader of the Sfakiots, a merchant by the name of Daskalojannis (Teacher John), is skinned alive. Uprisings continue into the 19th century.

1821–9 Crete participates in the War of Independence, during which large parts of Greece are liberated.

1850 Chania becomes capital.

1866 Under siege from the Turkish military and in a hopeless position, Cretan freedom fighters and their supporters from mainland Greece blow themselves up in the Arkadi Monastery.

1896–7 Crete is liberated with the help of the western Great Powers but the British insist that Crete adopts a position of independence under a High Commissioner.

Modern Crete

1898 Prince George, second son of the Greek monarch George I, becomes High Commissioner of Crete (until 1906). The Cretan lawyer, Eleftherios Venizelos, becomes the leader of an alliance which seeks union with Greece.

1909 Venizelos becomes Prime Minister.

1913 After the Balkan Wars, Macedonia and Crete are united with Greece. Crete enters World War I on the side of the Entente. Venizelos, leader of a liberal, anti-monarchist party, is in and out of office until his defeat in the election of 1932, when he returns to Crete.

1919–23 An expansionist policy towards Turkey continues but a Greek attack leads to a catastrophic defeat. Under the 1923 Treaty of Lausanne, Greeks in Turkey and Turks in Greece are repatriated. Some 22,000 Turks leave Crete, but 34,000 Greeks arrive to take their place. The town of Nea Halikarnassos near Heraklion is built to accommodate the refugees.

1936 General Metaxas heads a 'monarcho-fascist' dictatorship. Greece remains neutral over the Spanish Civil War and at the beginning of World War II. Venizelos dies in exile in Paris.

1940 Mussolini's Italy attacks Greece. The attack is repelled, marking the first defeat for the Axis Powers. Greece aligns itself with the Allies.

May 1941 Battle of Crete. German parachutists capture the island.

1941–5 German occupation of Crete. Two resistance movements are formed: one communist, one pro-British republican group. Many towns are reduced to rubble and the inhabitants shot.

1946–9 Greek civil war in which the communists oppose the restoration of the monarchy. In 1947 the Americans offer military assistance to Greece. In 1948 the communists are slaughtered in the Samaria Gorge and the monarchy is reinstated.

1967–74 Colonels led by Georgios Papadopoulos seize power in a putsch.

1972 Heraklion becomes capital of Crete.

1974–81 Dictators relinquish power. Conservative Nea Demokratia wins election.

1981 Greece joins the European Community. Socialist PASOK party under Andreas Papandreou ousts conservatives.

1990–3 Nea Demokratia returns to power led by Konstantinos Mitsotakis.

1993 Papandreou's PASOK re-elected.

Eletherios Square, Heraklion
Preceding pages:
Chania's Venetian harbour

No shortage of sights
Dining on Venizelos Square

Route 1

★ Heraklion

Half-finished concrete skeletons silhouetted against a blue exhaust haze, traffic at a standstill in barely adequate narrow streets – these are the first impressions a visitor receives of Heraklion (pop. 135,000), the starting-place for most new arrivals, and they are not very favourable. But spend just one night here and discover the hidden side, a more beautiful side: a quiet old town where stray cats snooze in the sun, shopping streets for locals rather than tourists, traditional *kafenia* and an authentic Cretan nightlife in one of the many *lyra* bars.

In addition, in and near Heraklion are Crete's two main tourist sights: the Archaeological Museum with its unique collection of Minoan artefacts and the Palace of Knossos.

History

Except for the years between 1850 and 1972, Heraklion has always been the capital of Crete. Nothing remains of the palace used by the Venetian governor-general and his Turkish successor. It was situated near the Lion Fountain.

Ancient Heraklion was named after Hercules, the Greek hero. When the Arabs conquered Crete in 828, they fortified the ancient town and named it Rabd el Kandak (Arabic for moat). The Venetians changed Kandak into Candia in 1204 and established the 'Duke of Candia' here. After a siege lasting 21 years (1648–69) Heraklion became the last Cretan town to fall into Turkish hands. After the annexation to Greece, Heraklion took on the apsect of a metropolis. In World War II the city suffered heavy bombing by both the Germans and the British. Now it is a 'mini-Athens', a place of refuge for those seeking work.

★★★ *Archaeological Museum of Heraklion* **❶**

(Tuesday to Sunday 8am–6pm; Monday noon–6pm).
For all those interested in the Minoan Civilisation, there can be no better place to start than the Archaeological Museum. The fact that the masterpieces of Europe's oldest civilisation are gathered here under one roof is rather unusual – many of the finest pieces from late Classical and Hellenistic Greece are scattered around the museums of the world. Why is Crete a special case? As in mainland Greece, it was teams of foreign archaeologists that conducted the first systematic excavations. British researchers opened up Knossos and the Diktaean Caves, Americans worked in Gournia, Italians in Phaistos, French in Malia. But these excavations started at the beginning of this century, long after the treasures of Greek antiquity had been shipped off to distant lands. Once Crete acquired independence in 1898 – it later became a part of Greece – the wholesale disposal of ancient finds was banned.

Minoan axes and sarcophagi

The museum is best visited in the afternoon, when it is quieter. Take a break in the museum garden café, but remember to retain the museum entrance ticket. It is impossible to see and appreciate everything, so select the most important exhibits such as those included below.

Gallery II: Early Palatial Period (2000–1700BC)

The wafer-thin 'eggshell vases' (Display 23), an example of Minoan potters' advanced skills, are quite remarkable. The ★★**Knossos Town Mosaic** (Display 25) showing the facades of the Minoan houses, the colourful paintwork and timber, is also of interest. This mosaic has given archaeologists an idea of how the buildings in Gournia once looked and the English archaeologist Arthur Evans used it to help him with the reconstruction of the Palace of Knossos *(see page 20)*.

Gallery III: Early Palatial Period (2000–1700BC)

Archaeologists have still not been able to decipher the ★★**Phaistos Disc** (Display 41). The characters which spiral inwards towards the centre in rows divided by incised lines resemble Egyptian hieroglyphics. Ideograms include a head with a 'punk-style' haircut, a flying bird and a man running in short trousers.

Gallery IV: Late Palatial Period (1700–1450BC)

The bare-breasted ★★★ **Snake Goddesses** (Display 50) were probably priestesses disguised as goddesses. Their waists are tightly belted, but their dresses are full. Snakes are entwined around their heads, bodies and outstretched hands. The snakes are thought to symbolise the barely controllable power of the earth and nature and, as snakes shed their skins, rebirth.

Snake Goddess

Gallery V: Late Palatial Period

Near the back wall of the gallery stands the **Model of Archanes**, a reconstruction in miniature of Minoan country houses and town villas with balconies and courtyards.

Gallery VII: Late Palatial Period

A display here shows the three famous relief-carved serpentine vases from Agia Trianda: The ★ **Boxer** vase shows a boxing scene and a jumping bull; the athlete is pierced by the bull's horn. The ★★ **Harvester** vase shows a procession at harvest time with the workers cheerfully singing as they carry sheaves of corn over their shoulders; one man stumbles and another turns his head mockingly. On the ★ **Chieftain**, an underling pays tribute to his master; what could be animal skins – borne by three men – are presented to him. Magnificent examples of the goldsmiths' work include the ★ **Bees of Malia** (Display 101), a pendant in which two bees are holding drops of honey in a honeycomb. The sweetness of honey was much prized and it would have been a very valuable commodity.

Bees of Malia

16

Gallery VIII: Finds from Kato Zakros (Late Palatial)

Display 109 houses a superb rock crystal *rhyton* (drinking vessel in the shape of an animal head). Another vessel in Display 111 shows a mountain shrine with goats, an image which has been recreated on the wall. The black ★ **Bull's Head** (Display 116), another *rhyton* but one whose mouth serves as a spout, is particularly impressive.

Upper Floor (Frescoes)

The Minoan frescoes in Galleries XIV–XVI all date from the Late Palatial Period. In many cases only fragments were found and the paintings have had to be restored. Arthur Evans is responsible for the grand-sounding names.

In Gallery XIV on the wall opposite the Procession Fresco from the west front of the Palace of Knossos is the ★ **Bull Leaping Fresco** (No. 14). Three stages of the jump are shown, or is it three different jumpers performing together? In the first jump, a woman seizes the charging bull by the horns, in the second a man somersaults over the bull, while the third shows the conclusion of the jump. After a pirouette, a woman with raised arms comes to a standstill. Spanish bullfighters maintain that such spectacular leaps are just impossible, so it remains unclear whether the bull leaps represent a ritual or a sporting act. It is quite likely that they symbolised both.

In the middle of the gallery stands the famous painted ★ **Chest of Agia Triada**. On one long side, priestesses are sacrificing a bull while a man with a flute provides a musical accompaniment. On the other long side, women pour some sacrificial liquid into a vessel which stands between

Chest of Agia Triada

two double axe stands. On the right a procession of three
men carrying animals and a model of a boat move towards
a white-clad, armless figure. A god? A death ritual? No
one has been able to say for certain what it represents.

Adjacent to the gallery exit stands a **wooden model**
of the Palace of Knossos. It shows clearly the full extent
of the structure.

On the left in Gallery XV is the **Miniature Fresco**.
Some feminist researchers argue that it proves Minoan society was matriarchal. Women with raised hands, probably priestesses, are performing a ritual, perhaps celebrating
the manifestation of a god, while the men look on ap-
provingly. A few yards further on stands ★ **La Parisienne**.
Evans likened this lumpy-nosed and large-eyed Minoan
woman to the ladies of Parisian high society.

La Parisienne

The ★ **Blue Monkey** (Gallery XVI) among papyrus and
lotus plants was formerly known as the 'Saffron Gatherer'
as Evans had arranged the fragments in the form of a man
picking crocuses. But the Greek archaeologist N Platon
rearranged the pieces to make a monkey.

Sights

Daedalou ❷ is a pedestrianised shopping street with
plenty of jewellery and souvenir shops, several good *tavernas*, pizzerias, ice-cream parlours and cafés. It joins
Venizelos Square ❸ with its Lion Fountain, sometimes

Venizelos Square

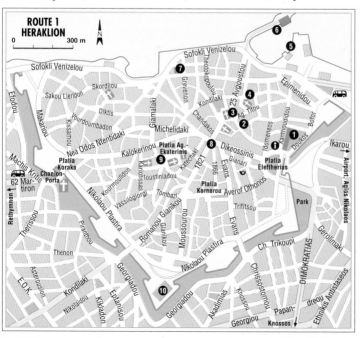

ROUTE 1
HERAKLION
0   300 m

called the Morosini Fountain. This peaceful, three-sided *platia* is a meeting place for the youth of Heraklion who at 'volta' time meet up with their friends by the *leontaria* (lions). Built by the Venetians in 1239, the former **Cathedral of Agios Markos** opposite is named after St Mark, the patron saint of Venice. The basilica is also used as an exhibition hall for copies of famous frescoes from some of Crete's churches. The **Venetian Loggia** ❹ was built in 1628 at around the same time as the fountains. It was used by the Venetian noblemen as a sort of gentleman's club and architecturally it is a fine example of a Venetian villa in Palladian style. The porch is now decorated with medallions of various famous Cretans, including Minos Kalokarinos, who first discovered Knossos, El Greco and his tutor Michael Damaskinos, the poet and Nobel prizewinner Odisseas Elitis, the writer Vitzenzos Kornaros (baroque poet and author of *Erotokritos*) and Nikos Kazantzakis.

Church of St Titus

Behind the Loggia stands the **Church of St Titus**. It is something of an architectural mix as a Turkish domed mosque was later converted into a Christian Orthodox church. Severely damaged by the eartquake of 1856, the building was finally renovated in 1972. The arabesques, ogee arches above the windows and the stalactite vaulting in the narthex are Islamic. Treasures inside include the iconostasis and the skull of St Titus in a golden vessel.

Fishing boats and tourist yachts use the old **Venetian harbour** ❺ and it is well worth taking a look inside the Venetian arsenal. After dark the illuminated **fortress** ❻ (Monday to Saturday, 8.30am–noon, 4–6pm) makes a fine spectacle when viewed from the quayside cafés. Three sculptured lions of San Marco can be seen on the exterior walls. Theatre performances are sometimes held in the inner courtyard.

Venetian harbour and fortress

The **Historical Museum** ❼ (summer: daily 9.30am–1pm, 3–5pm; winter: daily 8.30am–3pm) occupies the once grand home of the wealthy businessman, Minos Kalokairinos who discovered Knossos in 1878. It houses artefacts and displays from Crete's late-Classical period to the present day, and is well worth a visit. The upper storey documents the atrocities of German occupation from 1941 to 1945. Other exhibits include the study of the famous novelist, poet and dramatist Nikos Kazantzakis, including a collection of various editions of his books. Best known for his novel *Zorba the Greek*, Kazantzakis is also remembered in the museum at Mirtia near Archanes and the Folklore Museum in Agios Georgios on the Lassithi Plain *(see page 40)*.

Heraklion's **market** ❽ is located in Odhos 1866 and the narrow lanes nearby. Fruit and vegetables, souvenirs, *tavernas* and craft shops create a bazaar-like atmosphere. Sample Cretan yoghurt from clay pots, get your shoes repaired on the spot or buy some herbs and spices at very reasonable prices. At the upper end of the street, by the **Platia Kornarou**, stands the Venetian **Bembo Fountain** with its headless Roman statue from Ierapetra. The Turkish fountain beyond is now a 'mini' *kafenion*.

The market has a bazaar-like atmosphere

19

On the **Platia Agia Ekaterini** ❾ stands the 16th-century **Church of Agia Ekaterini**, the former church of the St Catherine Monastery (Monday to Saturday 9.30am–1pm; Tuesday, Thursday and Friday also in the evening 5–7pm. Closed Sunday and public holidays). At the time of the 'Cretan Renaissance' it was used by the Venetians from the St Catherine Monastery on the Sinai peninsula as a religious college. Now it is mainly of interest for its **collection of icons** by Michael Damaskinos painted in Italo-Byzantine style.

There are two other churches on St Catherine's Square, both named after the soldier saint Minas, the patron saint of Heraklion. The larger Classical 19th-century church has been the town's **Cathedral** since 1895. In the 1980s a new set of frescoes was commissioned and the paintings follow the usual Byzantine pattern with the Passion sequence in the vaulting and the saints on the lower walls. The smaller **Minas Church** dates from the 15th century. Worth seeking out here are the superb 18th-century gilded iconostasis with grape tendril patterns, and some valuable icons.

Minas Cathedral

Minas Church, iconostasis

Kazantzakis' grave ❿ is to be found adjacent to the **Martinengo Bastion**. A wooden cross marks his last resting place, and on his gravestone is inscribed the poignant message which epitomised his life: 'I hope for nothing. I fear nothing. I am free.' It is not surprising that Kazantzakis frequently clashed with the church, as hope (for redemption in paradise) and fear (of God) are important articles of faith.

Route 2

★★★ Knossos

Knossos: detail

Knossos, the grandest of the Minoan palaces lies 7km (4 miles) outside Heraklion amid the vineyards of Kefala hill. The No 2 bus leaves Heraklion for Knossos every 20 minutes. Open Monday 8am–noon, Tuesday to Friday 8am–6pm, Saturday, Sunday and public holidays 8am–3pm.

The excavation and publicity owe much to one man: Arthur Evans. This 43-year-old English archaeologist came to Crete in 1894, not to excavate Knossos, whose existence had been proven in 1878 by a Cretan businessman and amateur archaeologist, Minos Kalokairinos, but in search of a pre-Greek script. Evans was a man of many talents, having already worked as a newspaper reporter, travel journalist, ethnologist and museum director, but Knossos intrigued him. He wanted to match the status of

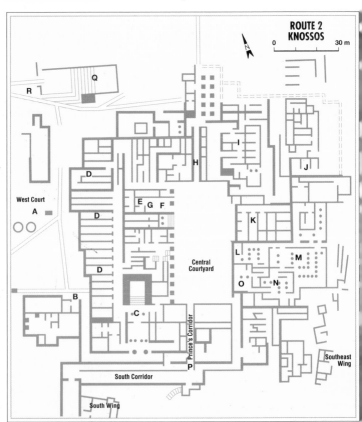

**ROUTE 2
KNOSSOS**

0   30 m

N

Q

R

I

H

J

D

West Court

A

E G F

D

K

L

M

D

Central Courtyard

O

N

B

C

Prince's Corridor

P

Southeast Wing

South Corridor

South Wing

Schliemann, the German archaeologist who had aroused considerable public interest by discovering the sites of Troy and Mycenae. When Crete attained independence in 1898, Evans' time came. As a wealthy man, he was able to purchase the land on which Knossos stood and a quickly-established trust, the Cretan Exploration Fund, contributed further cash. Digging began in 1900. The area of the palace was exposed in less than a year, much too quickly in fact, as a lot of important information was lost or inadequately documented.

Criticism was also levelled at Evans' attempts to create a 'romantic ruin'. While the Italians in Phaistos and the Americans in Gournia were content to simply expose the ruins, Evans rebuilt the palace with lots of reinforced concrete and painted it in bright colours. Some of the rebuilt sections were deliberately left incomplete. Observant visitors will discover that a moulding ends abruptly to create a dramatic impression, or that sacred horns and *pithoi* are set out together in an artistic arrangement.

The names for the rooms, such as the Hall of Double Axes and the Queen's Toilet were devised by Evans and used in his book *The Palace of Minos at Knossos*.

Knighted in 1911 for his work at Knossos, Evans died in 1941 at the age of 90.

Tour of Knossos

West Courtyard [A]. The bronze bust of Evans which stands on the right of the path by the palace entrance was unveiled in 1935 in his presence. The slightly raised Corridor of the Procession leads over the cobbled West Courtyard up a grand flight of steps to the Small Palace (on the other side of the road and not accessible). The circular walled ditches in the courtyard were probably used as a store for devotional offerings which had been removed from the palace shrines.

The Palace of Knossos

21

Idealised ruins – South Propylon

The Light Well

Fresco of dolphins in the Queen's Megaron

Only the reconstructed foundations of the **West Entrance [B]** and the *polythyron* complex remain.

The **South Propylon [C]** is an example of the idealised ruins mentioned above. A version of the large procession fresco adorns the wall – original fragments can be viewed in Heraklion's Archaeological Museum (*see page 16*). The Mycenean *pithoi* (storage vessels) nearby were left there by Evans to show that by 1450BC, in the Late Palatial Period, the Myceneans were already well established in Knossos.

A flight of steps leads up to the reconstructed *piano nobile* or upper storey. It offers a fine view over the ground floor and into the **storerooms [D]**. Separated from each other by strong walls, these rectangular rooms consist of box-shaped depressions, probably cool underground shelters for keeping tributes and bartered goods such as cloth, oils, cereals etc. Around the sides stand huge, tall *pithoi*.

Archaeologists have hung copies of well known Minoan frescoes on the walls of the **Light Well** and **'Lustral Basin' [E]**. There is also a fine view over the **terrace [F]**. The famous **Throne Room [G]** is not accessible, but it can be viewed through a wooden grille. The alabaster throne dates from the Early Palatial Period. Benches line either side of the room. Who sat on the throne and benches is something archaeologists and historians would dearly like to know. The fresco griffins flanking the throne are copies (originals in Heraklion Archaeological Museum) dating from Knossos' Mycenean era, i.e. after 1450BC.

A replica of the throne can be seen in an outer chamber. One advantage of displaying replicas is that visitors can 'audition' as Minoan kings or simply take a rest! Another replica is on view in the International Court of Justice in The Hague. In Greek mythology, King Minos was believed to be a wise judge.

By the **North Entrance [H]** stands a reconstruction of a splendid relief fresco with a charging bull.

Storerooms and workshops [I], **[J]** and **[K]**. Rather surprisingly, these rooms lie directly adjacent to the living quarters.

The **Grand Staircase [L]** leads down into the living quarters of the king of Knossos. Brightly painted shields hang on the walls.

The **Hall of Double Axes [M]** is so called because double axe symbols have been incised into the wall. Nearby lies the King's Megaron, a kind of conservatory.

The **Queen's Megaron [N]** has a bath tub behind a screen. Frescoes of Minoan ladies, a dancer and dolphins adorn the walls (originals in Heraklion Archaeological Museum).

The **Queen's Toilet [O]** uses a drainage system. When Evans discovered this room, he was said to have exclaimed: 'Now I am the only person on Crete to possess a toilet that flushes!'.

The **South Entrance [P]** to the inner courtyard is decorated with a copy of the *Prince of the Lilies* fresco – the only picture to portray a male figure in the whole palace.

The **Palace Theatre [Q]** is situated at the end of the **Corridor of the Procession [R]** which then leads down to the **Small Palace**.

The north entrance

Prince of the Lilies

23

Excursion to Archanes

The wine-producing village of **Archanes**, which can be reached by a bus leaving Heraklion harbour every hour, has a friendly and inviting atmosphere. It stands on the ruins of a Minoan palace, which came close to Knossos in terms of size and grandeur. The present-day village church was built on the cobbles of the palace's inner courtyard.

There are three important Minoan sites nearby: **Fourni**, set on a hill and a good half-hour's walk away from the town, is a large necropolis, which was used from the 3rd millenium to the time of the Myceneans. ★ **Vathipetro**, 3km (1¾ miles) south of Archanes, is a Minoan mansion dating from 1580BC. One of the buildings contains large storage jars and a wine press, proof that the vineyards of this area have a very long history. On the north slope of Mount Jouchtas, to the southwest of Archanes, **Anemospilia** is a temple where, in 1700BC, human life was sacrificed to ward off earthquakes.

Attendants will open up the sites for a small sum. Only Fourni is unattended.

In the middle of the village, to the right of the main street, artefacts from Archanes are on display in a one-room **museum** (daily 8am–2.30pm, admission free). The story of human sacrifice at Anemospilia is particularly well documented.

Route 3

The Ida Mountains: ★ Heraklion – ★ Tilisos – ★ Anogia – Plain of Nida – Ida Mountains (35km/22 miles to Anogia, a further 20km/13 miles to the Plain of Nida)

This mountain tour starts in Tilisos with its Minoan villas and continues to Anogia, a large Cretan mountain village famous for its *lyra* players and partisans. Woven articles are produced here as in Kritsa (*see page 43*). A partly metalled road leads up to the Plain of Nida where in summer shepherds take their *mitata* (cheese-making equipment, pens and makeshift beds) and sleep under the stars with their flock. An ascent of Crete's highest mountain, Psiloritis (2,456m/8,050ft), is possible within one day from here. Two other worthwhile trips include a bridlepath walk across the mountains to Kamares or through the Rouvas Gorge to Zaros (each 5–6 hours).

Shepherds and sheep take to the hills

Several buses a day go to Anogia, but hire a taxi to reach the Nida Plateau from Anogia.

Unlike many of the other Minoan remains, those at ★ **Tilisos** (14km/9 miles) may be viewed in peace and tranquillity. The site lies beneath pine trees and all that can be heard is the drone of the cicadas. So far only three villas from the Late Palatial Period have been excavated (Houses A, B and C). More houses, probably the homes of the poorer villagers, lie underneath present-day Tilisos.

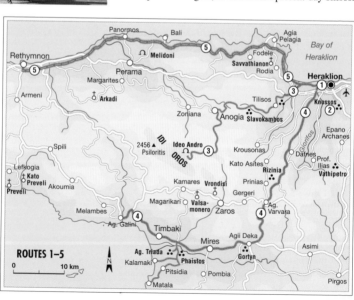

ROUTES 1–5

0   10 km

The cemetery, usually the place for the most interesting finds, has not been found yet.

The villas show all the hallmarks of Minoan architecture: monumental entrance halls with *polythyra*, lustral basins, pillared crypts and storerooms, not to mention the flushing toilets (see House A).

Minoan villa at Tilisos

Observant visitors will see that the villas are often constructed on older foundations dating from the Early Palatial and Pre-Palatial Period. At the northeast corner of Villa C, however, a large round cistern with steps intrudes into the light well, indicating that alterations were made later on by the Myceneans. A few yards to the west of the cistern stands a Classical altar in a shrine. The earliest settlement lasted well into Dorian times, a period of at least 1,500 years.

The village of Tilisos itself is a fairly primitive village where wine production is the main occupation. The compact, circular *platia* is a restful spot from which to observe Cretan village life. Few tourists venture into these parts.

The road to Anogia passes through a ravine and to the left of the ravine's entrance lie the remains of a Minoan villa at **Slavokambos** (22km/14 miles). Spiridon Marinatos, who later acquired fame after uncovering Minoan Akrotiri on Santorini, discovered the ruins and initiated the dig. A *polythyron* and a pillared crypt can be identified, but the otherwise poor condition of the excavations is attributable to German soldiers from World War II who destroyed the walls.

25

The mountain village of ★ **Anogia** (pop. 2,500; 34km/ 21 miles) nestles on the slopes of the Ida Mountains at an altitude of 700m (2,296ft). In summer, the clear mountain air comes as a welcome relief after the sweltering heat of the lowlands. The road into the village passes along a beautiful avenue and up to the town hall and church square of upper Anogia. In the square, a statue of a soldier with sabre and musket serves as a memorial to those who died in the rebellions against the Turks in 1821 and 1866.

The square in Anogia

On both those occasions the village was destroyed and then rebuilt. But the cruellest event in Anogia's history happened within living memory. By the summer of 1944, the German forces were in retreat on all fronts. Partisans in Greece, and particularly on Crete, were anxious to speed up their departure. British forces and Cretan resistance fighters pulled off a spectacular feat, when they abducted the German Commander-in-Chief, General Kreipe, and smuggled him off the island, passing through Anogia, over the Ida Mountains to Preveli, from where he was taken to Alexandria in Egypt. The livestock farmers of Anogia played their part in the escapade by helping to hide the abductors. In the three weeks between the abduction and the eventual evacuation, the Germans deployed no less than

Anogia – a place to escape the heat

Anogia is famous for its woven goods

30,000 men in the vain search for the general. In reprisal for this humiliation, on 15 August 1944 the village was burnt to the ground by German troops and all the men living within a radius of a mile from the village were rounded up and shot.

A memorial plaque by the town hall reminds visitors of the massacre and the order to burn down the village is engraved on an alabaster slab. The Americans played a major part in helping to rebuild Anogia after the war.

Music has an important traditional role in Anogia. Vassilis Skoulas, the late Nikos Xilouris and his brother Psarantonis (Fisherman Anthony), all famous *lyra* players, are sons of Anogia. Not surprisingly, *tavernas* entertain the tourists with organised Cretan evenings and the villagers will also try to sell their woven goods.

Allow a good hour for the 20 bumpy kilometres (12 miles) beyond Anogia to the **Nida Plateau**, where in summer the dairy herdsmen of Anogia set up a cheese-making plant. The metalled road leads to a **tourist centre** and then on to a car park where the ascent of **Psiloritis**, Crete's highest mountain, can begin. Allow between six to eight hours. The route is waymarked with red dots and cairns. Sometimes the path cuts across rough terrain, so sturdy shoes with ankle guards are advisable.

High up on the Nida Plateau

Situated near the tourist centre lie the **Idi Caves**, sacred to the Minoans and then adopted later by the Dorians as the birthplace of Zeus. His precise birthplace is often difficult to establish. Some thought he was born in the caves at Psyhkro in the Diktaean Mountains on the Lassithi Plain *(see page 40)*. Other places on the mainland have also been considered as possible sites, but priests often had an ulterior motive for such claims. Pilgrims would arrive bringing offerings and money!

Route 4

The Messara Plain: Heraklion – Agia Varvara (detour to Zaros) – ★ Gortyn – ★★ Phaistos – ★ Agia Triada – Agia Galini/Matala (70km/43 miles) *See map p24*

Many of Crete's most interesting sights are concentrated within the Messara Plain: the Minoan palaces of Phaistos (Festos), Agia Triada and the Roman capital of Gortyn. The ruins of Gortyn lie among olive groves so a visit there will involve a good walk. Finish the day with a refreshing dip in the Libyan Sea near Matala or Agia Galini.

The journey starts with a tour through the wine-producing region around Heraklion (Malvasier) and up through the pass near Agia Varvara. The road branches off here to Zaros and Kamares, following the southern slopes of the Ida Mountains from where there is a splendid view over the Messara Plain and the Asteroussia Mountains. Sample some of the local trout in Zaros and then stroll through the green Rouvas Gorge, whose clear mountain streams feed a lake and the Zaros trout farm.

Vineyard near Heraklion

With some careful timing the tour of the Messara Plain can be accomplished using scheduled buses, although it is obviously more convenient to take a hire car, in which case more time can be allowed and a detour to Zaros included. On Saturday there is a lively market in Mires.

Near the village of Prinias on the right of the road just as it approaches **Agia Varvara** (30km/19 miles), lies a plateau where the city-state of **Rizinia** once stood. Objects found here are in the 'Daedalic style' and rank among the most valuable of the exhibits in Heraklion Archaeological Museum. It is worth taking a walk around the site, not because of any ruins but for the view. Agia Varvara itself lies almost exactly on the watershed between the north and south coast. An old Cretan saying goes: 'whether the sun is shining on the north coast or the south, it will always be raining in Agia Varvara'. An interesting folk museum with exhibits such as traditional farming tools is situated on the right of the main road through the town.

The church in Agia Varvara
A comfortable pace

★ **Zaros** (pop. 3,500; 15km/9 miles) lies at the entrance to the Rouvas Gorge. Walkers can follow a good path, with railings in places, from a reservoir with a *taverna* as far as a picnic site beneath kermes oaks (about 5 hours there and back). The **Agios Nikolaos Monastery** appears after an hour's walk. This is the only monastery in Greece where the Julian calendar is still used and it accommodates both monks and nuns but in separate buildings.

Devotees of Byzantine art will find plenty to interest them in the churches of Valsamonero and Vrondisi. The paintings are in the Italo-Byzantine style of Venetian Crete.

Ask a local

In front of **Vrondisi Monastery** stands a Venetian fountain with Adam and Eve under the tree of paradise. Four spouts of fresh spring water, symbolising the four rivers of paradise, flow down. The only monk in the monastery will explain that the Turks 'beheaded' Adam and Eve. He will also show visitors a room which has photos documenting the important part played by the monastery in resisting the Turks and the German occupation.

The nearby village of **Vorizia** was destroyed by German troops in 1943. Here, visitors should obtain a key from the custodian to the church of **Agios Fanourios**, all that is left of the enormous monastery complex of ★ **Valsamonero**. The interior of the church is richly decorated with frescoes. These 14th- to 16th-century paintings are regarded as the most significant examples of Byzantine art on Crete. One of the paintings shows the rarely illustrated *akathistos-hymnos*, a song of praise to Mary which is sung 'not seated' (Greek = *akathistos*). Other frescoes show scenes from the life and death of John the Baptist.

The monasteries are linked by a path through the gorge, but the attractiveness of the walk has been spoilt by refuse which has been tipped into the gorge from the road above.

Amphitheatre and ancient olive trees at Gortyn

The ruins of the Roman capital of ★ **Gortyn** (45km/28 miles) (summer: daily 8am–7pm; winter: daily 8am–3pm) lie to the left and right of the road to Mires. The city is fenced off and an entrance fee is payable but a visit is well worth it. A walk outside the site can also be very enjoyable as it is possible to climb the acropolis hill and look for the Imperial Roman monuments among the olive trees. Paths lead to a theatre and a stadium, a number of shrines and the huge, excavated site of the Roman praetorium.

Tour of the ruins

Only the altar remains from the **Church of Titus [A]**. This 6th/7th-century cathedral had three naves and a dome and was the last resting place of the apostle Titus, who remained on Crete to spread the Christian word after Paul left the island. After Crete's Arabic period (961), Gortyn was abandoned. Heraklion was adopted as the new capital and another church of Titus built there.

Church of Titus

The **Odeion [B]** houses stone blocks inscribed with the 'Code of Gortyn', Europe's first known legal code. These blocks were found built into the rear supporting wall of the Roman odeion and are sometimes described as the 'Queen of Greek Inscriptions'. Dating from the 5th century BC, they were originally displayed for public information on the Agora at Gortyn. The 600 lines of script are written in an archaic form of Greek. The letters of every second line are inscribed back to front so the text reads from left to right and then from right to left – a form of writing known as *boustrouphedon*, the Greek word for ploughing with oxen. The text details the civil and criminal law as it applied to the various strata of society. For example, a fine of 60 obols was imposed for adultery among slaves, while freemen could expect a fine of between 600 and 1200 obols. Marriage between slaves and freemen was possible and so was adultery. If a slave committed adultery with a freeman, he was fined twice as much as the freeman. If he was caught in the act, the amorous escapade would cost between 1,200 and 2,400 obols. To put these sums into context, it needs to be understood that a manual worker, whether freeman or slave, earned at that time between three and six obols per day, although a slave would have to give a large part of his earnings to his master.

The Code of Gortyn

29

The **plane tree [C]** is a rare example of an evergreen plane (platanus orientalis cretica) – according to mythology, the place of the sexual union between Zeus as a bull and Europa. The wedding night is said to have lasted a hundred years and the offspring of this liaison were Minos and his brothers Rhadamanthys and Sarpedon. The **theatre [D]** has not yet been excavated. There is a fine view of the surrounding area from the **acropolis [E]**.

In the eastern part of the site is the **Shrine of Isis and Serapsis [F]**. In order to secure their rule, the Romans often simply adopted the religion of their subjects, in this case the Egyptians. Other examples of Roman architecture which lie nearby include a **theatre [G]**, a **nymphaeum [H]** with a praetorium (seat of the governor), **baths [I]**, an **amphitheatre [J]** and a **stadium [K]**.

A popular mode of transport

The main staircase at Phaistos

Mires (53km/33 miles), a dusty, unattractive place, is the main town on the Messara Plain. Nevertheless, the Saturday market can be an interesting event with many of the farmers from the surrounding villages arriving by donkey.

Of all the Cretan palaces, the ★★ **Palace of Phaistos (Festos)** (63km/39 miles) is probably the finest (Monday to Friday 9am–5pm, Saturday and Sunday 9am–3pm). It is perched on the crest of a hill with a view over the broad Messara Plain and the Ida Mountains, which are capped with snow until well into spring.

The Italian archaeologists who have been digging here since the beginning of the century have, unlike Evans at Knossos, not resorted to concrete and paint. They have left the ruins as they found them, so that the visitor can distinguish between the Early and Late Palatial Periods.

Phaistos, like Knossos, raises many questions. Why does the palace here not have any wall paintings as at Knossos or even at the nearby royal villa at Agia Triada? Where do the wheel tracks, which are visible on the floor of the inner courtyard, go? What was the function of the royal villa at Agia Triada *(see page 31)*? The French archaeologist Paul Faure maintains that it is 'bourgeois thinking' to assume that the king would have had a summer residence only a few miles from his palace.

Old Palace
New Palace
Greek structures

PALACE OF PHAISTOS (FESTOS)

0   50 m

Tour of the ruins

The **West Court [A]** dates from the Early Palatial Period. After the catastrophe of around 1700BC, the new palace was rebuilt about ten yards to the east. The **pithoi [B]** (storage jars) of Early Palatial origin are kept under a concrete cover. The drains and basins beneath the vessels were to catch any spilt liquid. The **house walls and alleys [C]** are those of the Minoan town that once surrounded the palace. Like Knossos, Malia and Kato Zakros, the town is not separated from the palace by a wall. A cobbled path that runs through the maze of houses dates from the time when Phaistos was a Dorian city-state.

A broad staircase gives access to the **monumental entrance [D]**. The **throne room [E]** with the nearby lustral basin and storeroom resembles that at Knossos, but no throne has been found. In the **storerooms [F]**, some remarkable masons' markings can be seen on the antae of the separating walls. Many of the *pithoi* were rearranged by the excavation team. On the west side of the **inner courtyard [G]**, the outline of the inner courtyard of the Early Palatial Period can be made out as a series of blocks.

Other details of the palace meriting closer inspection include: the **lustral basin [H]**; the **bronze furnace [I]** with traces of clinker (fenced off); the **main entrance [J]** to the inner courtyard; the **Royal Chamber [K]**, luxuriously fitted out with a wall covering of alabaster tiles, *polythyra* and light well, and the **chambers [L]** where the Linear-B tablets and the Phaistos Disc were found. The palace archives may well have been stored here.

Agia Triada

At ★ **Agia Triada**, 4km (2½ miles) from Phaistos, is another Minoan palace (daily 9am–3pm, Saturday and Sunday, 9am–2.30pm), but some archaeologists regard it as a villa for the ruler of Phaistos. The complex dates from the Late Palatial Period. The Myceneans constructed a megaron (main hall) on the foundations and then built a town and market place near the palace. Even in high season, it remains quiet here, with the incessant droning of cicadas in the tall cypresses the only sound to be heard.

Matala and **Agia Galini** are the best known seaside resorts on the Messara Plain. Coach loads of visitors descend on the two towns in the afternoon having spent the morning visiting Phaistos and Gortyn. In Matala it is worth taking a look inside the many caves that pepper the rockface by the beach, giving it the appearance of a Swiss cheese.

Matala

More peaceful than Matala or Agia Galini are the villages of **Kalamaki** and – 3km (1¼ miles) inland – **Pitsidia**. Backpackers often make for here, staying in cheap rooms and then making the 3km (1¼-mile) walk along the footpath to the beach at **Kommos**.

Route 5

North coast west of Heraklion: ★ Heraklion – Rodia – ★ Fodele – Margarites – ★ Arkadi – ★★ Rethymnon (80km/50 miles not including detours) *See map p24*

View of Heraklion from the mountains

The road westward out of Heraklion runs through wild, mountainous terrain and the coast drops steeply down to the sea. Hotels and beaches are only to be found in one or two bays, such as Agia Pelagia, Fodele, Bali and Panormos. It is worth making the occasional detour. A few miles beyond Heraklion near an oil-fired power station, the road branches off to the mountain village of Rodia. Here a footpath leads to the convent of Savvathianon, an oasis of peace in an attractive flower garden. Fodele, the birthplace of the painter El Greco, lies in a fertile valley of orange and lemon plantations. Margarites is noted for its pottery which is still made using traditional methods. The Arkadi Monastery in an isolated spot on the plain is a symbol of Cretan opposition to the Turkish yoke.

If it is only possible to spend a day on the detours to Rodia, Fodele and Arkadi, then a hire car will be necessary, but Rodia, at least, can be reached quite cheaply by taxi from Heraklion. A bus service links Fodele with Heraklion and three or four buses a day connect Arkadi and Rethymnon (*see page 50*).

The only power station on Crete is situated 10km (6 miles) outside Heraklion close to the beach. It is powered by diesel oil and cooled by brackish spring water that flows out of the limestone. The mountain village of **Rodia** with its houses clinging picturesquely to the hillside is about 5km (3 miles) from here. The ruined villas, some with

Traditional pottery at Margarites

Gothic window and door frames are an impressive sight. They are the former residences of wealthy Venetians who appreciated the splendid view over to the island of Dia, Heraklion and the round bay.

Four kilometres (2½ miles) above Rodia stands the convent of **Savvathianon**. It can only be reached by following a winding footpath up the hillside. At the end of World War II, the monks' monastery was abandoned and the building was destroyed, but nuns from all over Greece vowed to keep the convent functioning and they have clearly succeeded. Water gurgles from the spring and irrigates a beautiful garden which is lovingly tended by the nuns who are always happy to welcome visitors. They offer a guided tour around the buildings starting in the monastery church, on through the garden into St Anthony's Chapel and finally into a reception room where coffee or *raki* is available. One way of recompensing the nuns for their time is to buy one of their delightful crocheted or embroidered bedcovers. Alternatively make a small contribution towards the upkeep of the building.

Savvathianon Convent

Agia Pelagia (25km/16 miles) is a modern, faceless resort in a bay of the same name and much favoured by package tour operators.

Detour to ★ Fodele

Turn off the main road 26km (16 miles) from Heraklion and after a further 3km (1¾ miles) the village of **Fodele** appears. Fodele is famous as the birthplace of Domenikos Theotokopoulos, better known as El Greco. The village lies in the heart of a green orange plantation by a stream that never dries up even at the height of summer. A short, signposted walk crosses the stream to a ruined house, near the locked mid-Byzantine domed basilica in the abandoned hamlet of Loubinies. It was here that the painter renowned for his Mannerist style first saw the light of day. On the *platia* at Fodele stands a bust of El Greco and there are several shops selling woven products. A memorial in Toledo stone donated by the University of Valladolid and dated July 1934 also pays tribute to the 'immortal fame of Domenikos Theotokopoulos'.

Fodele – birthplace of El Greco

Bali (45km/28 miles) is a small fishing port and resort which has so far managed to resist the main tour companies and has no large hotels although there are a lot of small pensions. The independent travellers who stay in Bali meet up in the *tavernas* which are clustered around the picturesque harbour.

Bali

Only 3km (1¾ miles) from Bali along a narrow country lane is the grotto of **Melidoni**. The pottery village of **Margarites** is a little further inland and is well worth a visit. Here, all kinds of pots are made, in particular the large storage *pithoi* which were known in Minoan times. Many of the goods produced in the studios are destined for the souvenir shops and the skilled potters here would have no work were it not for the island's buoyant tourist trade. Further attractions of the village include the church of Agios Ioannis Prodromos with its beautiful 12th-century frescoes, as well as the church of Agios Georgios with its expressive painting of the Virgin Mary.

Arkadi Monastery can be reached from Margarites. First make for Eleftherna (on the site of an ancient city – the watch tower is in good condition and can be seen from a distance) and then follow a metalled road for 5km (3 miles) to Arkadi. For an easier route keep going on the main road to Rethymnon but take a left turn 5km (3 miles) before the town and follow a winding road through the gorge and then up the mountain side as far as the plain.

Arkadi Monastery

★ *Arkadi Monastery*

The monastery at Arkadi is a byword for heroism in the long struggle for Cretan independence. In November 1866, when the monastery – which had become a focus for the resistance movement and was also a haven for refugees – was faced with annihilation at the hands of Turkish besiegers, the abbot in charge ordered the gunpowder magazine to be blown up. His decision caused the death of nearly a thousand Cretans – men, women and children – and almost as many of the Turkish adversaries. The event drew worldwide attention to the plight of the Cretan freedom fighters but the Great Powers were preoccupied with their own problems at the time. The British adopted a *laissez faire* policy towards the Ottoman Empire for fear of encouraging Russian expansion into the Mediterranean. It was 1897 before independence was granted, but 9 November is now a national holiday when the martyrs of the independence struggle are remembered.

Skulls of the martyrs

A mausoleum was erected on what is now the car park in 1910 and a display cabinet contains the skeletons (mainly skulls) of the martyrs. In the monastery itself, the refectory on the left-hand side still exhibits many of the battle scars. The roof of the gunpowder magazine was blown off in one piece and a plaque (in Greek) makes reference to this fact. On the right near the monastery is a small museum (nominal entrance fee charged) which documents the struggle of 1866. A number of icons, costumes and ritual objects are also on display.

St George icon

The monastery church dates from the 15th and 16th centuries and has a most elegant facade built in the Creto-Venetian style with twinned composite pillars and capitals. The interior was badly damaged and the icons that decorate the church now are of 20th-century origin. The iconostasis is carved from olive wood and dates from 1927.

Route 6

North coast east of Heraklion: ★ Heraklion – Chersonisos – Malia – ★★ Palace of Malia – ★ Agios Nikolaos (70km/44 miles)

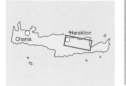

This is an area of Crete that belongs to the major tour operators. The less attractive side of Crete is on view along the road between Heraklion and Malia. The building boom of the 1960s saw the rapid emergence of high-rises and huge apartment blocks, often beside a busy thoroughfare and interrupted only by restaurants and souvenir shops. No proper planning arrangements meant that the infrastructure for the summer influx was inadequate – there are still few adequate pavements.

Yet there are one or two highlights. The Palace of Malia remains one of Crete's most interesting sights, and between the palace and the sea lies a strip of unspoilt and protected coastline. The triangle of land between Sissi, Agios Nikolaos and Cape Agios Ioannis is even lonelier. Only the elderly and children live in the impoverished villages on this peninsula – any other able-bodied person will be working in the tourist centres. Milatos still exudes the atmosphere of a small fishing village, but without the tourists.

Service buses shuttle between Heraklion and Agios Nikolaos every hour. Anyone in a hurry will take the new road, while those who would like to see where many inhabitants of Heraklion live or spend their free time will follow the old road which follows the cliffs and the beaches as far as Gouves.

35

Beach bar with pool, Malia

Amnissos (8km/5 miles) was once the harbour for Knossos. The Minoans simply pulled their boats on to the sand. Nowadays the ruins of a Minoan villa sit uneasily alongside a go-kart track and a riding stables. It was in the house of the port commander that the famous lily fresco was discovered. It is now one of the highlights of the fresco gallery in Heraklion's Archaeological Museum.

Another fresco in rather better condition was found at a Minoan villa near **Nirou Chani** (14km/9 miles) on the main road. The archaeologists were astounded to discover a large number of bronze axes here. Several of them are now on display in Gallery VII of the Heraklion Archaeological Museum.

Some fine beaches much favoured by the local people line the coast between these Minoan remains, including the state-run EOT beach near **Karteros** – entrance fee covers shower, changing cubicles, parasol and a lawn – and the narrow beach at **Tobruk** which has a good, cheap fish restaurant. Buses to Tobruk which make a detour to the EOT beach leave from the Platia Eleftherios in Heraklion every 20 minutes.

A torch is advisable for anyone planning to visit the grotto at **Eileithyia**. Take the road to Episkopi 8km (5 miles) from Heraklion and then turn left after 1km (½mile). In Minoan times the 62-m (200-ft) deep cave was visited by pregnant women paying homage to the resident fertility and mother god in the hope of a trouble-free childbirth. Eileithyia means something like 'she will come (to your aid)'. The immigrant Dorian Greeks simply incorporated the goddess into their system, believing her to be the daughter of Zeus. For Christians, the *Panagia* or Virgin Mary undertook the role as guardian of pregnant

A solitary stretch of beach

36

The road to Episkopi

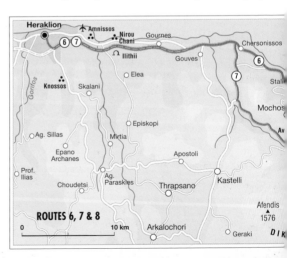

women. In order to visit the cave, a pass has to be obtained from the Heraklion Archaeological Museum.

About 20km (12 miles) beyond Heraklion to the left of the main road near **Gouves** lies an American base. The soldiers rarely set foot outside the base in uniform and do not travel in convoys through the countryside. The fact that the Americans keep a low profile is an indication that the Cretans view their presence with some suspicion.

Chersonisos (26km/16 miles) was once a quiet little fishing port – its full name is actually Limin (Port) Chersonisou. In the winter it is a ghost town, but in summer it is a mecca for package holidaymakers with hotels and all the shops close to the tourists' hearts. There may be some enthusiasts of early Christian art among the summer visitors, in which case a visit to the two **floor mosaics** is essential: one is to be found within the grounds of the Nora hotel and the other is fenced off near the harbour. Cretan folk art is celebrated at the private **Lychnostates museum** which is situated some 500m (¼ mile) from the town centre (daily except Monday, 9.30am–2pm).

Malia (43km/26 miles) is another package tour destination, but the village has not lost its old heart. To the right of the main road are the church, *platia* and some attractive old houses. On an island just off the sandy beach stands the white chapel of Agios Nikolaos, the patron saint of mariners. Take care when bathing here as there are some treacherous undercurrents. Every year tourists drown in these dangerous waters.

★★ *Palace of Malia*

The third biggest Minoan palace lies 37km (23 miles) from Heraklion and is situated just off the main road between

Beach at Chersonisos

Tasty morsels at Malia

37

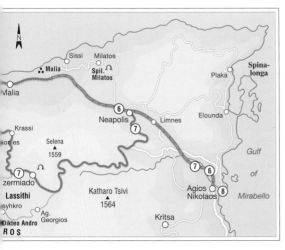

olive groves and the unspoilt north coast. A French archaeological mission has been digging here for many years stopping only during and shortly after World War II. In recent years the living quarters at Malia have been excavated and opened up to visitors, and they are in better condition than any of the other palace ruins. EU funds have been provided for the construction of wooden covers to protect the remains from rain and tourists' feet.

Buses run between Heraklion and Agios Nikolaos approximately every hour, stopping by the road which leads to the palace. Continue on foot for about 1km (½ mile). Open daily 9am–3pm.

The Kernos

A **West Court** with raised processional ways.
B **Storeroom section** with four round corn silos.
C The **Kernos**, a ceremonial stone slab with 34 small depressions around a central hollow where Minoans presumably made votive offerings of seeds, bread, wool or olive oil to a fertility goddess.

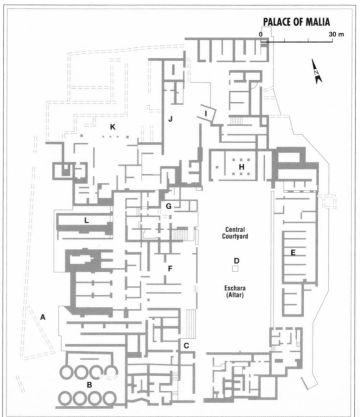

PALACE OF MALIA

0   30 m

N

J I
K
H
G
L   Central
          Courtyard
          E
F   D
          Eschara
          (Altar)
A
C
B

D The **Inner Courtyard** of the palace with a brick hearth (*eschara*) in the middle for roasting meat.
E **Storeroom** with *pithoi*.
F **Pillared crypt**, a shrine.
G **Throne room** where some valuable finds were discovered including a sceptre with a panther's head, now on view in Heraklion's Archaeological Museum.
H **Hall** with strong pillars thought to have been used as a kitchen.
I **Alterations** made by the Myceneans.
J **Northern Courtyard** with storerooms to the north and east.
K **Living quarters** with garden.
L **Storeroom**.

Pithoi near the north entrance

To the north of the palace lies a collection of buildings which the French archaeologists termed the Agora as it seemed to resemble the market place of the Greek city-states. Also of interest is a sunken area *(crypte hypostyle)* surrounded by benches, but its precise function remains unknown.

A pleasant walk leads from the palace across the fields, down to the coast and then on to Sissi. Nearby are the ruins of the *chrissolakkos* (pot of gold), the cemetery for the Palace of Malia. It was here in one of the graves that the famous honeybee pendant was found. Copies can be seen in all jeweller's shops, but the real thing is on display in the Heraklion Archaeological Museum. The nearby marshland is a breeding ground for many species of birds.

At **Neapolis** the road from the Lassithi Plain joins the National Highway to Agios Nikolaos (70km/43 miles) *(see Route 8)*.

39

Archaeological exhaustion

★ Heraklion or Agios Nikolaos to the ★★ Lassithi Plain (45km/28 miles) *See map p37*

The alluvial plain of **★★ Lassithi** is famous for its white canvas windmills which pump up water from the wells to irrigate the fields – an excellent example of an alternative energy source at work. Unfortunately, electrically powered motors are increasingly replacing natural energy. There are some fine walks to be enjoyed up into Diktaean mountains, including, possibly, a climb to the cave where Zeus was born. If the summer heat becomes unbearable, then the clear mountain air of the upper plateaux will refresh and revive. There are rooms to let in every village.

There are two access roads, one from Heraklion and one from Agios Nikolaos. Both take their time to snake up the hillsides to the pass which offers a fine view over the plain. All the villages lie on the edge of the plain so that none of the fertile soil is lost to roads and houses. Potatoes, vegetables and fruit are the main crops.

A service bus leaves Heraklion in the morning and returns later in the afternoon. From Agios Nikolaos, the bus returns immediately so it is better to hire a car.

If arriving from Heraklion, then take a short detour to the gnarled **plane of Krassi**, to enjoy a locally-produced *raki* from the *kafenion* under the biggest plane tree on Crete or else sample the spring water from the Venetian fountain opposite. A stop at the **Panagia Kera** is also worth considering. The frescoes which date from the 14th century resemble those in the Kritsa Panagia (*see page 43*).

The **★ Diktaean Cave** at **Psyhkro** is thought to be the most likely site of Zeus' birthplace. This sacred Minoan grotto with stalactites and stalagmites extends 70m (230ft) inside the mountain. The cave is damp, however, and the steps can be very slippery. Engaging a knowledgeable guide may be advisable; there is usually no shortage of qualified candidates waiting at the car park, from which the entrance to the cave is about a 20-minute walk. The guides and donkey drivers also sell candles, but a torch is preferable.

The **Agios Georgios Folk Museum** (daily 10am–4pm) is housed in a fortress-like 19th-century house in the nearby village of the same name. It was built without windows as Turkish attacks were a serious threat at that time. The museum displays traditional agricultural and domestic utensils from the anvil to the loom. One room in the museum is dedicated to the life and work of Crete's great novelist and poet, Nikos Kazantzakis.

Lassithi is famous for its windmills

The Diktaean Cave – birthplace of Zeus?

Agios Georgios Folk Museum exhibit

Route 8

Agios Nikolaos harbour

★ **Agios Nikolaos**

Agios Nikolaos (pop. 8,000), a village founded in 1869, is not surprisingly the most popular place in Crete. Landscape and position are unique: a peninsula washed by the clear blue sea, a picturesque freshwater lake with a channel linking it to the harbour, a long promenade with bathing beneath the cliffs, the pretty offshore islands of **San Antonio** and **Spinalonga** and then finally **San Nicolo Bay** where Venetian boats once anchored. Two luxury hotels, Minos Beach and Minos Palace now occupy prime locations in the bay.

Holidaymakers in search of sun, beaches and plenty of nightlife plus all the comforts of a modern hotel will feel at home in Agios Nikolaos. In the summer, tourists mill around Lake Voulismeni with its restaurants, discos and cafés. In winter only the locals' *tavernas* stay open.

Buses for Heraklion, Kritsa, Sitia and Ierapetra leave Agios Nikolaos every hour. Twice a week ferries leave for Piraeus via Santorini and Rhodes via Karpathos. There are also day trips to the island of Santorini.

History

The bay was originally a harbour for the nearby Doric mountain town of Lato and was called 'Pros Kamares' (To The Arches). The name Agios Nikolaos derives from the church of St Nicholas (near Minos Palace Hotel). Parts of the church date from the iconoclastic period. The Mirabello fortress on the peninsula was built dur-

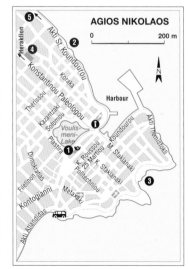

ing the Venetian occupation, but its remains now lie buried beneath the hotels. The seaward side of Agios Nikolaos protected the Spinalonga fortress.

Agios Nikolaos is the administrative centre for the regional council of Lassithi. All the main sights in eastern Crete can be visited by bus from the town.

Sights

Lake Voulismeni

Local nightlife is centred around **Lake Voulismeni** ❶ and the harbour. The lake is almost round, and according to myth, the goddess Artemis bathed in it. Once a freshwater lake, it was connected to the sea via a channel constructed between 1867–71. A similar geological phenomenon – a freshwater lake near the sea fed by an underground spring – can be seen near Kournas in western Crete (*see page 54*).

The **peninsula** ❷ is the site of the 13th-century Venetian Mirabello fortress, of which hardly a trace remains. It is illustrated in Venetian engravings.

The **beaches** ❸ at Agios Nikolaos can get very crowded. Other beaches are to be found beneath the coast road in the direction of Elounda. Water quality is very good as the town is equipped with a sewage plant.

42

Taking it easy

The ★ **Archaeological Museum** ❹ (Tuesday to Sunday 8.30am–3pm) houses important finds from eastern Crete. In Room V, a skull with a coin between its teeth attracts a lot of interest. The coin was to pay the ferryman for the journey across the River Styx to the kingdom of the dead.

In the **Church of Agios Nikolaos** ❺, a rather unprepossessing Byzantine domed church, fragments of frescoes from the iconoclastic period (726–843) with aniconic, i.e. non-human motifs, have been preserved. The reception at the Minos Hotel keeps a key to the church.

Excursions

Elounda and Spinalonga

Elounda, a resort close to Agios Nikolaos, is famous for its luxury hotels and the picturesque bay enclosed by the island of Spinalonga. It is considerably less crowded and more laid back than Agios Nikolaos, and the cafés and restaurants near the harbour are great places to sit and watch the world go by.

The name **Spinalonga** (which means long thorn in Italian) refers not only to the off-shore peninsula, which is linked to the mainland by a causeway, but also to the famous fortified island on its seaward side. Caïques leave every day from Agios Nikolaos and Elounda. Sometimes extended trips are organised to include beach barbecues or swimming above the ruins of **Olous**, an ancient village near Elounda where remains of houses can be seen just below the surface of the water.

The fortified island of Spinalonga is dominated by its **Venetian fortress**, one of several which defended the Cretan north coast. The others are Gramvousa and Souda in the west. Spinalonga was built in the 16th and 17th centuries with the siege tactic used by the Ottomans in mind, and it was never conquered. Even after Crete was firmly in Turkish hands, a Venetian guard remained on the island until 1714. It was finally withdrawn when its strategic value in a Turkish controlled Mediterranean ceased.

A number of 20th-century houses lie abandoned on the island. These were once part of a leper colony that the Greek government established in 1903 once the Turkish settlers had been expelled. The lepers lived here until 1957 and were given access to a school, laundry, shops, workshops, even a *kafenion* and a cinema. A disinfection centre for friends and relatives was situated near the old jetty opposite **Plaka**. The victims of leprosy were buried in concrete coffins in a cemetery near the present-day harbour.

Spinalonga Island and fortress

The remains of the leper colony

★ *Kritsa*

Every day in summer bus loads of tourists arrive to see this 'typical Cretan village' of whitewashed houses spread across a hillside beneath a steep rockface. The village women lay out their inexpensive weaving and crochet work for the tourists. In the triple-naved Byzantine **★★ Panagia Kera Church** just below Kritsa, the fine 13th/14th-century frescoes are in excellent condition. At that time Crete was ruled by the Venetians and consequently considerable Italian influence is in evidence. The Catholic saint, Francis of Assisi, for example, can be seen on the north pillar of the main nave. Note the annotation FRA-ZEC-KO.

Different styles suggest a number of artists who probably worked at different times. In the central nave, the style

The Dorian city of Lato

is clearly linear, traditional and hieratic, whereas in the south nave, the figures seem more animated and lifelike. In the central nave, the Passion sequence is depicted with a gruesome representation of the Bethlehem child murder, while the south nave paintings show episodes from the story of Anne, Mary's mother. In the north nave, alongside the church's founders in grand Venetian costume, stands an artist's impression of the Last Judgement with scenes from hell and paradise.

Lato

Set in an outstandingly beautiful position on a mountain ridge amid wild landscape 3km (1¼ miles) north of Kritsa is the former Dorian city-state of **Lato**. It was founded in the 7th and 8th centuries BC, and is a typical double settlement of a fortified town set on two hills within sight of the port. Its most important period was probably during the 3rd and 4th centuries BC, when it expanded in area as well as population.

Between two acropolis hills stands the **Agora**. An *exedra*, an outdoor platform for meetings and discussions, occupies a shady position under an evergreen chestnut oak. Opposite, a flight of steps leads down to Latos' **administrative buildings** with benches, a table and then a watchtower to both right and left. The commercial centre was situated to the left beneath the Agora. Mortars, hand mills and cisterns can be seen in the basements of the houses.

A local observer

Take a taxi up to Lato and then follow the bridlepath on the other side of the hill down to **Chamilo**. At around 3pm (check exact time) a bus leaves for Agios Nikolaos. There is a pleasant *taverna* in Chamilo.

Route 9

Eastern Crete: Agios Nikolaos – ★ Gournia (detour to Ierapetra) – Sitia – ★ Toplou – ★ Vai – ★★ Kato Zakros (120km/74 miles)

A good road winds its way from Agios Nikolaos (*see page 41*) around the Gulf of Mirabello to Sitia, offering en route some of the finest panoramic views in all Crete. Far below the road the sea glistens in the sun and the white houses of Agios Nikolaos shimmer in the Aegean haze. The offshore islands of Mochlos and Psira were once important Minoan settlements.

Beyond Sitia the picture changes. The vegetation becomes sparse and the landscape takes on a slightly lunar appearance despite the gently rolling hillsides. For miles around, the scene is one of desolation. Abandoned, crumbling houses tell of a population that has fled from the land to Heraklion, Athens, Europe, the USA or Australia in search of work.

The palm beaches of Vai and the area around the Palace of Zakros at the entrance to the 'Valley of the Dead', a fertile region with banana plantations, have an oasis-like quality and in high season they can be very crowded. Other interesting sights on this route include the Minoan Pompeii at Gournia, the quiet, Venetian harbour town of Sitia and the fortified monastery at Toplou.

The tour can be completed by scheduled bus services but it would be advisable to allow two days with an overnight stop in either Sitia, Palekastro, Zakros or Kato Zakros. Please note that the buses only descend to Kato Zakros in the summer months. At other times the service terminates at Upper Zakros (Pano Zakros).

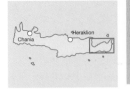

Gulf of Mirabello

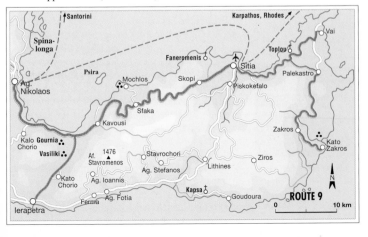

The ruins at Gournia

The village of ★ **Gournia** (19km/12 miles), or the Minoan Pompeii, lies on a hill close to the sea at the narrowest point of the whole island. A Minoan track once led across the island to the town of Ierapetra, 14km (9 miles) away on the south coast. If the main focus of interest in the other Minoan palaces centres on the royal families, here it is the everyday life of the ordinary people of the Late Palatial Period which dominates. Homes, workshops and shops have been uncovered. In the centre on a hill is a public square with larger buildings, perhaps the governor's residence, and a shrine nearby. Cobbled streets separate the blocks of tightly packed houses, often two or three storeys high. Cattle and stores were kept on the ground floor with living quarters above. Spaces in the walls indicate that timber frames were used in the construction. Here and there are troughs (*gournes*) in the floor for the cattle, hence the (non-Minoan) name.

Excavations at Gournia began at about the same time that Evans started work at Knossos. The leader of the team at Gournia was a woman by the name of Harriet Boyd-Hawes. At that time the world of archaeology was male-dominated and the arrival of a woman caused quite a stir. The whole world was captivated by Evans' work on the royal palace, while the discoveries made by a woman about everyday life some 3,500 years earlier were almost entirely ignored.

Detour to Ierapetra

The mosque at Ierapetra

Ierapetra (pop. 9,000) is Crete's fourth largest town and also the southernmost settlement in Europe. First impressions of a modern town with few attractions may be slightly misleading as Ierapetra turns out to be quite an attractive resort with an old town and mosque, a municipal beach where fishermen sit under the tamarisks mending their nets and plenty of relaxing *tavernas* to while away the time. It also has an imposing **Venetian fortress** dating from the 13th century as well as a small archaeological museum. The most impressive of the objects on display is a large limestone sarcophagus on which Cretan wild goats are depicted.

Visit the Venetian fortress…

Buses leave approximately every hour for Heraklion, Sitia, Mirtos and Makrigialos. Two buses a day follow the south coast route to Heraklion via Viannos. Fine beaches are to be found to both the east and west of Ierapetra. The quiet fishing and farming villages are popular with backpackers in the summer.

and then head for the beach

On a hill at **Fournou Korifi**, 2km (1¼ miles) to the east of **Mirtos** (12km/7 miles to the west of Ierapetra), lies an interesting excavation – the remains of a small town from the Pre-Palatial Period in which a clan of about 200 people lived together in a complex of 90 rooms. No 'manor house' has been found so it seems that the inhabitants lived at a time before the existence of any state control and presumably co-operated together in a form of commune. Walkers will enjoy a stroll through the Sarakina Gorge which at its narrowest point resembles the Samaria Gorge (*see page 62*). Access via Mili and Males.

47

　　Arvi, a comparatively wealthy village 42km (26 miles) west of Ierapetra, lies amid banana plantations and greenhouses at the entrance to a gorge. It can be reached more directly from Heraklion 82km (51 miles) away.

　　Keratokambos, 52km (33 miles) west of Ierapetra, is difficult to reach and receives few visitors. Accommodation is available in private rooms.

　　To the east of Ierapetra lies **Makrigialos** (25km/16 miles). Boats ferry passengers from Ierapetra and Makrigialos to the islands of Chrissi and Koufonissi where dunes overgrown with juniper, crystal clear water and fine sand create a 'desert island'. It is uninhabited but, even so, no place in Crete is complete without a *taverna*.

Back on the main route, the road from Gournia to Sitia passes the viewing platform at **Agios Nektarios** (33km/20 miles). It offers a fine panorama across the **Gulf of Mirabello** with the blue sea shimmering below. Opposite stand a chapel and a restaurant. Try some of the cool, fresh drinking water from the nearby spring.

　　Sitia (pop. 8,000; 73km/45 miles) is a restful place with nothing of any special interest and only coarse sand beaches. Even in high season, few tourists find their way here. The town centre is situated around the *platia* by the harbour where a few cafés and *tavernas* can be found,

Panorama across the gulf

Flowers in bloom

Icon detail at Toplou

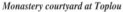

Monastery courtyard at Toplou

while the scanty ruins of a Venetian fortress known as Kasarma (Italian: *casa di arma*) look down over the town. A provincial archaeological museum on the road out to Piskokefalo houses finds from the locality, while a folk museum on the road to Agios Nikolaos (Therissou 13) displays old farming implements, domestic objects and woven fabrics.

Regular buses from Sitia run to Vai, Zakros and Heraklion from the station in Odhos Itanos. Ferries leave twice a week for Karpathos, Rhodes and Piraeus via Santorini.

The fortified monastery at ★ **Toplou,** (94km/59 miles) lies in the uninhabited 'lunar' landscape of the wild east of Crete. The name for the monastery derives from the Turkish word *top* which means 'cannon'. In the monastery church hangs an unusual icon with 61 small scenes rendered in the most exact detail. The style is reminiscent of naive paintings by the Dutch artist Breughel. It is titled: 'Thou art almighty, Lord' (Greek: *Megas o kyrie*). A shop outside the monastery sells icon reproductions and there is also a café, which is never short of passing trade as Toplou is firmly on the itinerary of the tourist buses to Vai and Kato Zakros. Crete's first wind farm has recently been built just above the monastery.

★ **Vai** (105km/65 miles) has a beautiful sandy beach which is very popular with day trippers during the summer months. Accommodation in Vai is hard to find as it is a protected area on account of a rare species of palm tree, *phoenix theophrasti*, named after the philosopher Theophrastus who mentioned it in his writings. Crete is

the only part of Greece where this type of palm grows wild. The locals of Vai maintain that this date palm 'forest' sprouted when Roman soldiers seeded the area – in passing – with date stones. It is a wonderful beach for children, as it slopes gently and the waves are not strong. To the north of Vai there are more beaches which are just as beautiful but have no facilities and so are much quieter.

The road from Vai to the Palace of Kato Zakros via Palekastro passes through one of the driest and therefore poorest regions of Crete. Many villages look deserted, the former inhabitants now living in Heraklion, Athens or Sydney. Where people do remain, then they will be the young and the old. The only exception is the village of Pano (Upper) Zakros which owes its relative prosperity to the tourist trade and a spring.

The water flowing from this spring has taken thousands of years to form the **Valley of the Dead**, so called because the Minoans buried their dead in the caves. Do not miss the chance to walk through this vast canyon. The entrance is 3km (1¾ miles) from Pano Zakros and the path is way-marked with red dots. It will take about two hours to follow the course of the stream down to the banana plantation by Kato Zakros Bay. Turn left here for the ★★ **Palace of Kato Zakros** (118km/73 miles), the fourth excavated Minoan palace. There are others but they have not yet been completely cleared.

At one time the palace lay by the sea, but the coast line has shifted about 800m (875yds) further east as a result of silt from the stream that flows through the 'Valley of the Dead'. From an economic point of view, the eastern end of Crete enjoyed a favourable position in ancient times. Egypt and the Near East were within easy sailing distance and many of the finds such as ivory teeth and other exotica reflect Kato Zakros' central position on the early trade routes. Unlike the other palaces, there had been no earlier building. It was constructed in the Late Palatial Period and then like all the others was destroyed about 1450BC. It shows all the typical features of a Minoan palace: inner courtyard, lustral basins, storerooms, pillared crypts and *polythyra*. Unlike Knossos, the residential section of the palace compound has been completely excavated.

What has surprised the archaeologists is the huge number of water basins within the site. In one of them well preserved olives about 3,000 years old were found. A bronze smelting furnace was discovered at the entrance. Close examination revealed that it was fitted with inlet and outlet vents which enabled the supply of air to be controlled. Alternate layers of charcoal and ore were piled into the furnace and then the liquid metal flowed from a spout on the opposite side of the vents.

Palm beach

The Valley of the Dead

Palace of Kato Zakros

Route 10

★★ Rethymnon

Rethymnon's lighthouse and beach

★★ **Rethymnon** (pop. 25,000) competes with Chania (*see page 56*) for the title of the prettiest resort on Crete. A worthy challenger indeed: the old town is better preserved and more compact than Chania and the Venetian port is smaller and more intimate. Fishing boats bob gently up and down in the water and fish restaurants line the quay in front of the pastel-washed house fronts. Narrow alleyways divide the houses into blocks which separate the Venetian houses with their Gothic-arched portals and stone-framed windows from the timbered Turkish houses whose balconies jut out over the street. The minarets, easily visible from the citadel, are reminders of Rethymnon's Turkish past. Rethymnon is the only Cretan resort to overlook a wide sandy beach and it has consequently become popular with those holidaymakers who enjoy sea and sand but who like to be near a bustling town.

Buses for Heraklion, Chania, Agia Galini and Preveli/Plakias leave from Odhos Moatsou (usually every hour). Buses to Anogia and the Amari district leave from Platia Iroon by the beach. The 'Arkadi' ferry leaves for Piraeus four times a week. There are also day trips to Santorini.

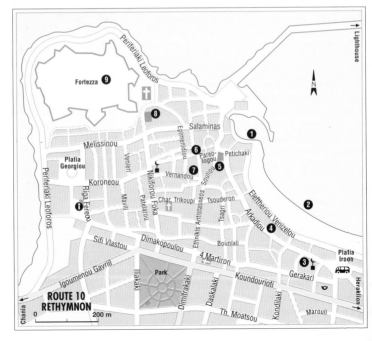

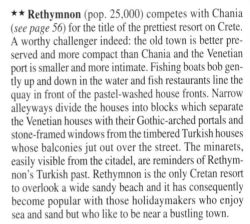

ROUTE 10
RETHYMNON

0   200 m

The Venetian harbour

History

Heraklion is Crete's principal economic centre, Chania is its political heart, but Rethymnon is the focus for the island's spiritual and scientific movements.

It is no accident that the town houses the arts faculty of the University of Crete (founded in the 1970s). Some earlier academics, who emigrated to Italy where they made a name for themselves, originate from Rethymnon. The most famous of them is Markos Mousouros (known in Italian as Marco Musuro) who worked with the celebrated Dutch humanist and Greek scholar Erasmus.

The oldest remains in the town date from Minoan times. Later to become a Dorian town, its pre-Greek name was Rethymna. After Constantinople was conquered by the Crusaders, Crete fell to the Genoese and was then sold to the Venetians who developed the town and built their harbour and the mighty Fortezza. During Turkish rule, Rethymnon was occupied mainly by Turks, and their leisurely lifestyle, which revolved around the coffee house and horse's saddle, is described graphically by the 20th-century writer Pandelis Prevelakis, a native of Rethymnon, in his novel *Chronicle of a Town*.

51

Sights

With its intimate, sophisticated atmosphere, the town's main attraction is undoubtedly the **Venetian harbour** ❶ Most of the fish restaurants have rather expensive menus.

The town's EOT Tourist Information Office and an exhibition of Cretan handicrafts are housed in a pavilion near the **beach** ❷.

Look out for the attractive flower garden by the 17th-century **Kara Moussa Pasha Mosque** ❸.

Odhos Arkadiou ❹ is *the* shopping street with leather goods among the best bargains. At the north end of Arkadiou, the narrow **Souliou** with some more interesting shops

Seafood at a harbour restaurant

Bargain sandals

The Venetian Citadel

The Rimondi Fountain

branches off to the right. A herb shop at No 58 offers a tremendous range. An icon painter works nearby as does a shoemaker who will make shoes to order.

Like its counterparts in Heraklion and Chania, the **Venetian Loggia** ❺ served as a gentleman's club for the Venetian well-to-do.

According to an inscription, the **Rimondi Fountain** ❻ dates from 1629. It supplied water to the townsfolk much like the Morosini Fountain in Heraklion. Underneath the name A(lvise) RIMONDI stand Corinthian columns and lion head waterspouts.

The **Pasha Nerazza Mosque** ❼ (Tuesday to Saturday 9am–3pm, Sunday 9.30am–2.30pm) was formerly the church of Santa Maria. Now it is the *odeion* or concert hall. Like many other buildings on the island, its changing function reflects Cretan history. The 16th-century Venetian monastery church was changed into a mosque by the Turks. The minaret offers a fine view over the town but a small entrance fee is required.

The **Archaeological Museum** ❽ in front of the fortress was once the Venetians' prison. As well as finds from the town and environs, artefacts from the Post-Palatial cemetery at **Armeni** are especially interesting. The grave chambers – now empty – may be viewed *in situ*. They are found 10km (6 miles) outside Rethymnon on the right of the road to **Preveli**.

The **Citadel** ❾ or **Fortezza** at Rethymnon was unique among the Venetian fortresses on Crete as it consisted of a fortress within a fortress. As well as the Venetians themselves, the local population were offered protection from invading forces. The munitions chamber, the cisterns and the **Sultan Ibrahim Mosque** with its broad dome are of particular interest. The top of the minaret was cut off by the Cretans, leaving only a stump.

Route 11

South of Rethymnon: ★★ Rethymnon – ★ Preveli – ★ Plakias (40km/25 miles) *See map p54*

Preveli Monastery lies in an isolated spot on barren rocky terrain 170m (558ft) above the Libyan Sea. A footpath leads down to Preveli Beach, once a secluded paradise frequented by backpackers and campers, but now a popular destination for sailors from Agia Galini and Plakias, although there are still no hotels. Plakias, another beach paradise, is found 15km (9 miles) further east, and the usual tourist facilities are available here. The town, situated at the foot of a valley, was, only a few years ago, a modest fishing village consisting of a handful of houses, but now there is a wealth of small hotels and pensions.

Several buses a day run from Rethymnon to Plakias. To visit the monastery at Preveli, leave the bus at Lefkogia and walk the last 6km (4 miles).

For a break from beaches and old monasteries, make a detour to **Spili** (turn right 22km/14 miles southeast of Rethymnon and continue for another 8km/5 miles). This attractive village owes its fertility to plentiful supplies of water. Good quality drinking water flows from a Venetian fountain with lion heads on the *platia*.

The main road to the south coast passes planes and carob trees in the Kourtalioti Gorge and the earlier monastery at Kato Preveli before arriving at the coast and curling round to the west to reach the 17th-century St John's monastery at ★ **Preveli** (35km/22 miles). This was another centre of resistance during the Turkish occupation and the rebellious spirit of the Cretans was revived again during the German occupation of 1941 to 1944. The monks helped to evacuate Allied troops after the Battle of Crete. In a thrilling escapade, the soldiers boarded submarines from the beach below. A memorial in the monastery testifies to the ferocious reprisals that followed. The monastery museum houses icons, costumes and ritual objects.

Preveli Monastery

The Kourtalioti river cascades down through a steep ravine and flows into the Aegean at ★ **Preveli Beach**. A freshwater lake has formed with date palms, oleander and eucalyptus on its banks.

Preveli Beach

★ **Plakias** has a long beach of the finest sand – undoubtedly one of the best on the island. With a sewage treatment plant at Plakias, the water is magnificently clean. Other beautiful but more isolated beaches are to be found: to the west about a 40-minute walk away, is Souda Beach and to the east, accessible from the road to Lefkogia, lie the beaches of Damnoni and Amoudi.

A moody view of Amoudi

53

Route 12

**The north coast between Rethymnon and Chania:
★★ Rethymnon – Kournas – Georgioupolis (detour
to Almirida and ★ Kokkino Chorio) – ★★ Chania
(75km/46 miles without detour)**

Jerakari Beach, 15km (9 miles) beyond Rethymnon, is the
longest beach on Crete. Crete's only freshwater lake at
Kournas is just a short distance (6km/4 miles) away. A
number of other resorts such as Almirida on the south coast
of Souda Bay are perhaps less well prepared for tourism.
Kokkino Chorio, a short distance inland, has been little affected by the advent of tourism and no overnight accommodation is available, but it is a good example of an old
Cretan village with bumpy, narrow alleys and traditional
architecture. Cacoyannis, the producer of the film *Zorba
the Greek,* declared that it was his favourite village.

An hourly bus service serves the villages on the main coast
road. Kokkino Chorio and Plaka, another pretty village,
can be reached by taxi from Kalives.

Lake Kournas

The almost circular **Lake Kournas** lies at the foot of the
steeply sloping White Mountains and is perfectly safe
for bathing. Pedalos can be hired and two *tavernas* on
the shores let rooms and offer authentic Cretan fare.

Georgioupolis (22km/14 miles) lies in the southwest
corner of Almirou Bay. To the north the cliffs of Cape Dra-

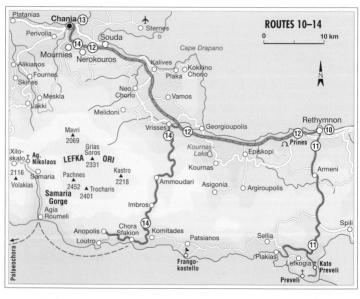

ROUTES 10–14

0 _____ 10 km

pano drop steeply into the sea while in the east the broad sands of Jerakari Beach disappear into the distance. The scene in Georgioupolis is quite delightful with an attractive *platia* shaded by tall eucalyptus trees. Fishing boats and yachts bob up and down at the mouth of the river.

Novice at Almirida Beach

55

Driving around the **Cape Drapano** peninsula is a pleasant way to pass a morning. The typically Cretan villages are now chiefly inhabited by elderly folk, women and children. The green, partly wooded landscape has that unspoilt beauty which many tourists appreciate. The fine beaches and fish restaurants at **Almirida**, a resort as yet undiscovered by the tour companies, are worth a look. Most of the visitors will be Cretans from nearby Chania. Opposite is the Akrotiri peninsula. In 1993, an interesting folk museum was opened in **Gavalochori** 5km (3 miles) away.

The road now runs high above the coast and on to Plaka and ★ **Kokkino Chorio**. The latter is sometimes described as the 'red village' after the blood that was shed in 1821 at the beginning of the War of Independence. Turkish troops drove 150 women and children into a cave below the village and murdered them. Despite modern developments on the edge of the village, Kokkino Chorio has been able to retain its rustic charm. A famous scene from *Zorba the Greek* in which the widow is stoned and Zorba intervenes was filmed on the *platia* outside the church.

The charms of Kokkino Chorio

During the German occupation Kokkino Chorio, at the entrance to the strategically important Souda Bay, was an important military base. Above the village, near the tiny Agios Georgios church, an underground bunker can be visited. Three galleries lead into the wood-panelled chambers underground. The older villagers maintain that there was even a cinema there. A cable railway ran from the tip of Cape Drapano to the bunker entrance.

Footpaths lead down to the few sandy coves beneath Plaka and Kokkino Chorio.

Local industry

Route 13

★★ Chania

To reach the centre of **★★ Chania** (pop. 70,000) can be a stressful experience. The cars and buses crawl through narrow lanes. It is no surprise to learn that Chania has the highest proportion of cars and buses per head in the whole of Greece. But it is worth all the delays and frustration as Chania town centre is a gem. The old town retains much of its charm with markets, bazaars and Venetian town houses, while the medieval picture postcard harbour, overlooked by restaurants and cafés, draws locals and tourists alike.

The old town

The suburbs of Chania have been laid out according to a plan. The roads meet at right angles with plenty of green spaces, even a park and a zoo – something of a rarity in Greece.

The old town, however, reflects years of changing occupation. Around the hill by the harbour, where there is evidence of a Minoan settlement, a jumble of pastel-washed houses and ancient ruins sit alongside each other. The Venetian palace in the Kastelli quarter, the *arsenali* or warehouses and, by the harbour, the Turkish Mosque of the Janissaries with its minaret complete the picture.

A Venetian stronghold

History

Known as Chania Kydonia in antiquity (*kydonia* means quince in Greek), the Venetians changed its name to La Canea when they won control in the 13th century. As a defence against the rival Genoese who plundered the town in 1266, the disgruntled Cretans and the Arabic and Ottoman threat, strong fortifications were built. The *castel vecchio*, built in the 13th century around the hill, was the first structure, but in the 16th century, a grander complex extending over a much wider area was created, consisting of slanting walls, heart-shaped bastions and a citadel at the entrance to the harbour. But despite the new defences, in 1645 Chania was captured by the Ottomans. It became their capital and retained this status until 1972 when the military junta passed the role to Heraklion, a town with a stronger economy. In 1913, after Crete became a part of Greece, the Greek flag was hoisted over the Firkas, the harbour citadel, for the first time.

Sights

The ★ **Market Hall** ❶ is a neoclassical structure based on the market hall in Marseilles. Inside, the full range of agricultural produce is on sale. The market was designed in the shape of a cross and the four arms of the cross are used for different types of produce. To eat a meal in the market *estiatorion* along with all the traders would be to experience the real Crete. The market hall is open during the usual business hours, ie it is closed on Monday, Wednesday and Saturday afternoon.

Skridlof 'Street of Leather' ❷ offers a wider range of leather goods than anywhere else on the island apart from Rethymnon. Leather boots will be made to measure, and you can even watch the cobbler at work. Service in terms of quality and quick delivery is guaranteed. There are also hand embroidered items, ornamental jewellery

Wedding cakes in Chania market

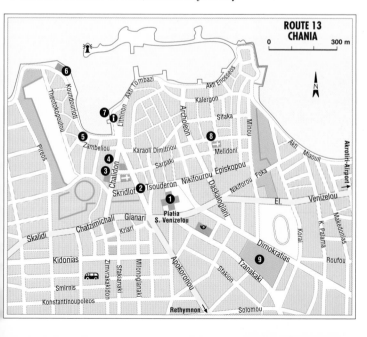

ROUTE 13
CHANIA
0   300 m

and ceramics. 'To Diporto' tucked away between the leather shops is an old-fashioned and cheap *kafenion-taverna* – a great place to watch the world go by.

The **Catholic Church** ❸ and Local Craft Museum in the inner courtyard exhibit Cretan woven fabrics and furniture. The opening times are irregular.

The ★★ **Archaeological Museum** ❹ (daily except Saturday and Sunday 9am–3pm) is housed in the Gothic **San Francesco Church**, the church of the Franciscan order. A minaret stump and washing fountain remain as evidence of its one-time function as the **Jussuf Pasha Mosque**. When Crete achieved independence and later became a part of Greece, the church was used as a cinema. When the Germans left in 1945, some of their military equipment was stored there. It was 1962 before it was converted into an archaeological museum.

Trot around town

Artefacts on display date from the Neolithic era to the Turkish occupation. The displays are all labelled. The Roman floor mosaic is beautiful, as is the seal – from the Minoan era – with a view of the town and a male weapon bearer. A colourfully-painted late Minoan clay sarcophagus depicts mountain goats and a deer hunt. The urns were found in the necropolis at Armeni.

Venetian patrician houses ❺ with attractive facades and portals can be seen in the narrow Odhos Moshou and the Zambeliou. The **Renieri Palace** and the former **Loggia** (No 43–45) are worth seeking out. The Latin inscription on the coat-of-arms: *nulli parvus est census qui magnus est animus* translates as 'nobody of great mind is poorly valued'.

The **Nautical Museum** ❻ (daily except Monday 10am–2pm) beneath the **Firkas** harbour bastion contains models of ships. Nautical equipment, illustrations of naval battles and photos document Greek maritime history. Room 3 contains an interesting collection of mussels.

The Venetian harbour

The ★★ **Venetian harbour** ❼ with the Mosque of the Janissaries and Venetian *arsenali* is where Greek families take their evening *volta*. Cretans wearing their best outfits parade up and down, show off their children and later meet up with friends or relatives in one of the many cafés. The picture postcard harbour could accommodate about 40 Venetian galleys. By the chapel of **Agios Nikolaos**, on the harbour mole opposite, both Venetians and Turks performed their executions and the bodies were then simply thrown into the sea. The **lighthouse** is a remnant of the years between 1830 and 1840 when Crete was handed over to Egyptian troops and exploited as a reward for the part they played in helping the Ottomans to suppress the rebellious Greeks. The **Mosque of the Janissaries** (permanently closed) is the oldest Turkish building in Chania. It was built soon after the Ottoman conquest in 1645. The

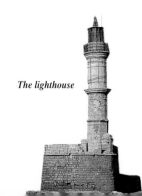

The lighthouse

58

Venetian *arsenali* serve as stores and workshops for fishermen and craftsmen. Many of them have been restored and are used for exhibitions.

Agios Nikolaos Church ❽ – San Niccolo in Venetian times – was converted into a mosque after 1645 and acquired a striking minaret. Reverting back to a Christian-Orthodox function in 1898, it was left unused except as a bell-tower.

In 1821 the Bishop of Chania, Melchisedek, was hung from the plane tree on the church square. This was described by the Turks as a 'preventative measure' as they feared a widening of the Greek uprising.

The **Municipal Park** ❾ and zoo were laid out in 1870 by the Turkish pasha of Chania in the style of European gardens. A few Cretan mountain goats peer out rather sadly from behind the fencing.

Excursion to the Akrotiri peninsula

The **Akrotiri** peninsula which juts out into the sea to the northeast of Chania is a good place to combine a tour of three monasteries with a walk through exceptionally beautiful countryside. An asphalt road leads from the **Agia Triada Monastery** with its Classical facade through a gorge up to the **Gouverneto Monastery**. A bridlepath, very steep in places, climbs seawards from this fortress-like building to the **Bear's Cave** with a stalactite in the shape of a bear. The cave and the abandoned ★ **Katholikon Monastery** are about an hour's walk away. A bold bridge construction across a gorge here is really rather impressive. A further 30 minutes away lies the sea and a chance for a dip.

The **grave of Eleftherios Venizelos**, Crete's best known politician, and his son Sofoklis lies above Chania on the way to Akrotiri. It was here that in 1897 the revolutionary committee met in the Elias Monastery under the leadership of Venizelos. Finally, in 1913, the demand for union with Greece was granted. All that remains of the monastery today is the little Sr Elias Church. Nevertheless, the view overlooking Chania and the Rodopos Peninsula is spectacular. A taxi is the best form of transport for this excursion. Ring for a one before your return journey from the Gouverneto Monastery (Chania taxi rank, tel: 58700).

The firing range at Akrotiri is occasionally the focus for protests by the Greek peace movement. The USA, Germany, Norway, Belgium, Holland and Greece use the site which is known as NAMFI (Nato Missile Firing Range) to test short-range rockets and air defence systems. To have so many foreign soldiers on Cretan soil – particularly Germans who once occupied Crete and killed many women and children – is a source of discontent among Cretans. Any NATO soldiers who leave their barracks wear civilian clothing and are asked not to draw attention to themselves.

Relaxing in the Municipal Park

Agia Triada Monastery

Route 14

South of Chania: ★★ Chania – Vrisses – ★ Imbros Gorge – Chora Sfakion – Frangokastello (85km/53 miles) *See map p54*

This route starts out towards Vrisses in the east and then crosses the island to the east of the White Mountains (Lefka Ori) and the Askifou Plain. Imbros is the starting point for a walk through the Imbros Gorge. Here the road clings to the steep slopes while, far below, a bridlepath follows the gorge floor. The road winds down to the quiet port of Chora Sfakion. In the afternoons tourists weary after walking the Samaria Gorge wait here for their transport back to the north coast. It makes a good base for excursions into the White Mountains or to the picturesque fishing village of Loutro, which can only be reached by boat. Sfakiots are famed throughout Greece for their brave resistance against occupying forces. The Venetians, recognising this, built two fortresses, one in Chora Sfakion and another 12km (7 miles) further east. The latter, Frangokastello, survives and is in fairly good condition.

The White Mountains

The route is well served by buses from Chania and Rethymnon. Frangokastello lies some distance from the main road and is best reached by taxi from Chora Sfakion. The bus from Chora Sfakion to Agia Galini stops at a road junction about 3km (2 miles) from Frangokastello, but it runs only two or three times a day.

Vrisses is situated at the junction of the north coast road and the road to the south. Huge plane trees dominate the *platia* on both sides of the river which flows into the sea

Backgammon in Vrisses

at Georgioupolis. Mountain cheese, yoghurt from clay bowls and fresh mutton are the local culinary specialities and supplies for the *tavernas* around the main square are delivered by the shepherds from the White Mountains.

From Vrisses the road winds its way up the Askifou Plain. Pass through Ammoudari and Askifou to reach ★ **Imbros**, the head of a gorge which many walkers choose in preference to the Samaria Gorge (*see page 62*). Access is from the end of the village beside a *kafenion* on the left side of the road. Until well into the 1950s this gorge was the only possible route to the south coast. To walk the gorge as far as the coast will take about two hours.

Even during the Turkish occupation **Chora Sfakion** (pop. 400) was an important trading centre. The Sfakiots owned many boats and they were able to continue trading unimpeded by the Turks. One of these merchants, Ioannis Vlachos or Daskalojannis (Teacher John), played an important part in the 1770–1 uprising against the Turks. He was assisted by the Russians who at that time were at war with the Turks. The uprising was quashed and Daskalojannis was skinned alive in Heraklion.

The ferry to Agia Roumeli

Chora Sfakion comes alive twice a day: in the morning when the boat to Agia Roumeli docks and in the afternoon when it returns. The morning's passengers are 'doing' the Samaria Gorge 'the lazy way' as the travel agents call it. This involves a walk of about two to three hours there and back but only as far as the Iron Gates. In the afternoon they return but in the company of those brave souls who have walked the full length of the gorge.

At other times Chora Sfakion is a quiet spot. *Tavernas* line the quayside and the water is crystal clear. Other destinations for walks into the hinterland include the mountain village of Anopolis and the coastal village of **Loutro**. The latter village is not accessible by car. The less energetic may prefer to visit it by boat.

Loutro

Frangokastello

The impressive fortress at **Frangokastello**, 16km (10 miles) from Chora Sfakion, is situated next to the sea. It was built in 1371 shortly after the Venetians had conquered the island. It looks at first sight to be well preserved but on closer examination it becomes clear that only the external walls remain. They are, nevertheless, an impressive sight. The sandy beach that it overlooks is one of Crete's finest. The flat coastline provides ideal conditions for children and non-swimmers as deep water suitable for swimming is a long way out. On the beach near the castle there is a *taverna*. Enquire at the other bars nearby about rooms.

If travelling by car to Frangokastello, take the road from Chora Sfakion to the village of **Komitades**. The church of **Agios Georgios** outside the village contains some well preserved Byzantine frescoes which date from the 14th century. At **Patsianos**, the road turns towards the coast.

61

The vast landscape

Route 15

★★★ **Samaria Gorge National Park** (★★ **Chania – entrance to gorge: 42km/26 miles, Chora Sfakion – Chania: 73km/45 miles**) *See map p64*

No holiday in Crete would be complete without a visit to the ★★★ **Samaria Gorge**. This ravine, one of the longest in Europe, has been a nature reserve and a Greek National Park since the mid-1950s. The threatened Cretan wild goat (*agrimi* or *kri kri*) has found a safe habitat here, as have many rare species of orchids and about 70 other plants which are unique to Crete. Ancient cypresses have survived centuries of deforestation.

Passing through the Iron Gates

Coach tours which include a walk through the gorge can be booked in Heraklion, Rethymnon and Chania. These day trips depart early in the morning for the Omalos Plateau, the starting point for the gorge walk. The passengers are picked up later on in the afternoon from Chora Sfakion (*see page 60*).

Fresh water spring

The walk through the gorge to Agia Roumeli on the coast covers a distance of 18km (11 miles) and takes between five and seven hours, according to fitness. Boats then ferry the weary walkers along the coast to Chora Sfakion (or Palaeochora in the opposite direction) between 2pm and 5pm. There is a charge for walking the gorge and the ticket must be handed in at Agia Roumeli where the park authorities check that all walkers have left the gorge by nightfall. Agia Roumeli has a number of restaurants and bars, but there are no snack bars or similar in the gorge. A water bottle is not necessary as there are plenty of places where cool, fresh water flows from the ravine walls.

The hike throught the Samaria Gorge begins at 1,100 metres (3,609ft) on the **Omalos Plateau**. In winter, the plateau, almost circular in shape, is flooded by water coming down from the surrounding mountains. Fortunately, the water can flow down the 2½-km (1½-mile) long **Tzanis Cave**. Legend has it that on moonless nights, a shepherd, enchanted by a water sprite, plays his lyre and sings of his sorrow at the mouth of the cave.

Just before the descent to the Samaria Gorge, there is a path leading to the Greek Alpine Club Hut. It lies at an altitude of 1,650 metres (5,423ft) and can serve as a starting point for treks into the White Mountains. The descent into the gorge itself is via a path still known as *Xiloskalo*, which means wooden ladder. The name is a reminder of the days when the only access to the gorge was by ladders. After about 4km (2½ miles) is the church of Agios Nikolaos and about 2km (1 mile) further on lies the abandoned village of **Samaria**, with its Byzantine church of Osia Maria the Egyptian. Samaria now serves as a base for the park wardens, but there is also a picnic site here and a telephone for emergencies.

The abandoned village of Samaria

The last 4km (2½ miles) are the most interesting and spectacular as the trail passes under high cliffs where all the sounds are magnified. When the wind howls through the narrow Sideroportes (Iron Gates), one can understand how tales of water sprites, demons and other strange creatures came about. The last stretch is extremely narrow, only 3 metres (10ft) wide with 500-metre (1,640-ft) vertical cliffs towering above. Through the gap, a broad valley stretches right down to the sea and Agia Roumeli.

Walkers prefering to experience the beauties of the gorge alone could consider three other options:

1 Arrive at Omalos in the evening and stay in the Xenia Hotel by the entrance to the gorge (reservation advisable, tel: 0821-93257) and then make a very early start the following morning.
2 Set off in the early afternoon, but before 3pm as the entrance to the gorge is closed then. Stay overnight in Agia Roumeli. There are plenty of rooms and a booking is not necessary.
3 Depart about midday, walk for two or three hours and then turn back.

The view from the ferry

Agia Roumeli derives its livelihood from the gorge and the crowds of walkers who arrive during the afternoon after the exhausting walk. Those who wish to stay the night can climb up to the Turkish fortress which once stood guard over the Libyan Sea and the shingle beach. Allow about 90 minutes.

Route 16

Western Crete: ★★ Chania – Maleme – Kandanos – Palaeochora (72km/44 miles)

To the west of Chania as far as Kolimbari and the Gonia Monastery (*see page 66*), hotel complexes occupy the narrow strip of land between the main road and the sandy beaches. This is the west Cretan centre for package holiday tourists.

At Maleme, the road turns to the south and passes through a relatively unspoilt part of Crete characterised by green and fertile countryside, although the reserves of woodland are badly depleted. Olives and citrus fruits are the main crops. Kandanos, up in the mountains, was destroyed by the Germans in World War II, while Palaeochora and the neighbouring coastal towns of Kountoura and Sougia are popular with backpackers.

The offshore island of Gavdos is the ideal spot for those seeking total tranquillity and isolation, a simple life and marvellous beaches. Boats leave from Palaeochora, Sougia and Agia Roumeli.

A cemetery near **Maleme** is the last resting place of the German soldiers who lost their life in the Battle of Crete. A British war cemetery is to be found near the harbour in Souda Bay (*see page 55*). Like Anogia in the Ida Mountains and many other places on Crete, in 1941 **Kandanos**

Memorial in Kandanos

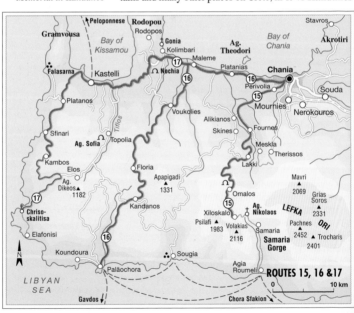

ROUTES 15, 16 &17

(pop. 1,000; 58km/36 miles) was destroyed by German troops and many of the inhabitants were murdered. This massacre followed the attempt of Cretan resistance fighters to hold up the German advance to the south coast. Two plaques in the square, one in German and one in Greek, serve as a memorial to the victims. In 1963 a German organisation which sought to make amends for Nazi terror built a waterworks for the town. It is located on the edge of the town and here, too, a memorial plaque in Greek and German recalls the events.

Palaeochora (pop. 1,500; 72km/44 miles) occupies an idyllic spot beneath a destroyed Venetian castle. There are no large hotels like those on the north coast, but there are a number of small pensions and most of the locals have rooms to let in their homes. Few tour operators include Palaeochora in their brochures, probably because it is too far from Chania airport. So most of the visitors to the town are independent travellers who appreciate the fine sand on the beaches, the walks and days out in this unspoilt part of Crete. Try the beaches at **Elafonisi** or **Sougia** or explore the peaceful mountain villages. Despite the remoteness, the nightlife in Palaeochora can be quite noisy, so avoid accommodation near the main street.

Religious flags in Palaeochora

65

From Palaeochora there are several buses a day to Chania and several boats each week to Sougia, Agia Roumeli, Loutro, Chora Sfakion and Gavdos.

Sougia is a small, remote village on the coast, situated at the end of a gorge between high walls of rock. It is a good deal quieter than Palaeochora and there are only a few small pensions, but private rooms may be rented. The overwhelming majority of holidaymakers in Sougia are young people.

Buses leave once or twice a day to Chania and there are ferries to Palaeochora and Agia Roumeli several times a week from May to September.

Gavdos, an offshore island due south of Chora Sfakion, is Europe's southernmost point. This distant island is car-free, has a population of about 45 and just one shop selling everything from shoelaces to brandy. Despite the southerly location, winters are cold and life can be tough on this windy island. The soil is poor and yet cereals have been harvested with a sickle here for over 2,000 years. At least the residents now have electricity, thanks to a solar energy plant and a wind farm. **Sarakiniko** is the best of the three beaches.

Boats leave from Palaeochora (4 hours) about four times a week and twice a week from Chora Sfakion (2½ hours). In the winter a post and supply vessel calls in at the island twice a week.

Sougia

Route 17

The west coast: Maleme – Gonia Monastery – Kastelli Kissamou – Chrisoskalitisa Monastery – Elafonisi (67km/41 miles) *See map p64*

This route follows the coast to the monastery at Gonia and then on to the small port of Kastelli. From here to Chrisoskalitisa Monastery and the lonely but beautiful beach by the Elafonisi lagoon, the route is difficult, particularly during the latter stages, but it is, nevertheless, worth making the effort.

Gonia Monastery: icon and visitors

Gonia Monastery lies on the outskirts of **Kolimbari**. The monastery church houses a valuable collection of icons, including a miniature of the Last Judgement on the left-hand wall. The picture shows well-known non-believers, such as the 'good kings' Darius and Alexander the Great, as well as the converted enjoying the pleasures of paradise. Low down to the right on the iconostasis, the 'Pillar Saint' Simeon Stylites can be identified. This Syrian ascetic is said to have spent 30 years preaching to the crowds from the top of a pillar.

The bodies of German soldiers killed in the Battle of Crete were kept at Gonia before burial in the war graves at Maleme (*see page 64*). Behind the monastery stands the Orthodox Academy of Crete which was founded in 1968. It holds seminars on subjects relevant to the lives of Cretans, such as the role of Cretan women or the effects of tourism on Cretan life.

Walkers will enjoy the rugged landscape on the uninhabited peninsula of **Rodopou** to the north. The sleepy village of Rodopou comes alive on 29 August for the Feast of John the Baptist. Mules and donkeys are laden with wine, *raki*, blankets, food, chairs and musical instruments. After a two-hour walk, the convoy reaches St John's Chapel situated in one of the lonely valleys of this uninhabited peninsula. A service is held in the chapel and the Bishop of Kastelli arrives to baptise any babies by the name of Jannis (John). Finally the time comes for celebrations to start. *Lyra* music begins and the festivities continue until daybreak.

Kastelli Kissamou

Kastelli Kissamou (pop. 3,500) is a small town where life proceeds at a leisurely pace. The locals earn their living less from tourism than from the land. The beach beneath the promenade is shingly and, compared to so many other Cretan beaches, has little to commend it. Kastelli harbour exports chestnuts harvested in the hinterland. The village of **Elos** is the centre of the chestnut trade and at the end of October the villagers celebrate the harvest with a 'chestnut festival' of music, dancing and feasting.

Ferries leave Kastelli two or three times a week to Piraeus via the Peloponnese (Githio and Kalamata). In high season there are cruises to Pirate Bay and the Venetian island fortress of Gramvousa.

There is a frequent bus service from Kastelli to Chania, once a day to the peaceful village of **Platanos**. There are a number of interesting icons in the church, one of which depicts the 99 Holy Fathers. From here one can visit the ancient city of **Falasarna**, which was the port for Polyrrhinia, an independent Minoan trading settlement. There is not much left of Falasarna now, but there are some deserted beaches and a couple of *tavernas*; it is also possible to rent rooms.

Chrisoskalitisa Monastery dates from the 17th century. Set on a rock above the sea with a rather fortress-like appearance, it is still used by a small group of nuns. Accommodation is available nearby in private rooms. For further information ask at the monastery (tel: 0822 61292). There is also a *taverna*.

Chrisoskalitisa Monastery inside and out

At **Elafonisi**, 6km (4 miles) south of Chrisoskalitisa at the end of a bumpy road, lies what is claimed to be Crete's finest beach. Despite a little oil pollution, the atmosphere here is South Pacific rather than Mediterranean. The sea shimmers blue, turquoise, green and all shades in between. It is possible to wade across to 'Stag Island' (Elafonisi).

In high season buses run to Elafonisi from Chania and Kastelli. Travel agents offer day trips. Enquire at 'Elafonisos Travel' in Chania (tel: 0821 45436). Tours include a visit to the **Agia Sofia Grotto** in the Topolia Gorge.

Waders at Elafonisi

Cretan Mythology

Chaos
In the beginning was chaos, from which Gaea arose to bring heaven, the sea and the mountains to the world. Gaea wedded her son Uranus and with him begat the Titans. Soon Uranus set himself up as ruler of the world, but his place was usurped by their youngest son, Cronus, who married his sister, Rhea. Frightened that his children would usurp his power, Cronus decided to swallow all his new born infants. But one of his children, Zeus, survived.

Zeus and Europa
Zeus, the father of the gods, was born in a cave and fed by three nymphs. When he grew up, he turned into a bull and abducted Europa, a Phoenician princess, from her home in Asia Minor. They spent their wedding night – it was said to have lasted one hundred years – under a plane tree in Gortyn. Their union produced King Minos and his brothers Radamanthys and Sarpedon.

Minoan bull

69

Minos, Pasiphae and the Minotaurs
Minos ruled Knossos and Crete and to the Greeks he was a wise ruler of the underworld. He had secured his king-ship by praying to Poseidon to send a bull to confirm his regal status, promising to then sacrifice it to the god. But he could not bring himself to sacrifice the beautiful ani-mal and as a punishment Poseidon made Pasiphae, Minos' wife, fall in love with it. She mated with the bull and bore the Minotaur, a half-man, half-bull monster. Minos kept the bull in a labyrinth.

Ariadne and Theseus
Ariadne, the daughter of Minos, fell in love with the Athen-ian hero Theseus. He had come to Crete to free Athen-ian hostages that the Minotaur kept under guard in the labyrinth. Theseus entered the labyrinth, killed the Mino-taur and, thanks to Ariadne's ball of thread, he was able to find his way out safely.

Daedalus and Icarus
Daedalus had been responsible for building the labyrinth where King Minos kept the Minotaur and he gave Ariadne the idea of using a ball of thread to help Theseus escape after killing the monster. For his treachery, Daedalus fell out of favour with King Minos and the vengeful king im-prisoned him in the labyrinth with his son Icarus. Father and son escaped, Daedalus having made wings so that his son could fly. Ignoring his father's warning, Icarus flew too close to the sun, the wax melted and he fell from the sky to his death.

Art History

Minoan Art

The Minoan civilisation is the Bronze Age civilisation of Crete that flourished from about 3000BC to about 1100BC. Its name derives from Minos, either a dynastic title or the name of a particular ruler of Crete who has a place in Greek legend. Reaching its peak about 1600BC, Minoan civilisation was remarkable for its great cities and palaces, and for its sophisticated art.

Architecture

Technically, Minoan civilisation was highly developed. Minoan palaces and the towns which surrounded them were all linked together with a network of tracks and paths. But Minoan Crete was not just a series of interlinked palaces. The network included smaller towns, and fishing and farming villages such as Gournia or Palekastro as well as shrines and country villas such as Tilisos or Vathipetro in central Crete.

What all the buildings have in common is a honeycomb-like pattern at ground level: a complex of tiny rooms, recessed and protruding facades, a maze of corridors and light wells. At Knossos there was even a sophisticated drainage system with three sets of pipes: one for spring water, one for rain water and one for waste. No wonder that the Greeks described this architectural style, which was after all in direct contrast to their own sense of symmetry, as 'labyrinthine'.

The walls of the houses and palaces were built with air-dried clay and sand and then reinforced with timber. Limestone blocks were, however, used at ground level and in the corners, while the interior walls were coated with clay and straw or else covered with alabaster tiles. The rough clay surface was sometimes finished with a fresco.

All the palaces had the following features in common: a central court and a western court where rituals and sporting events were held, perhaps the famous bull jumping ceremony or prayer sessions as shown in the illustrations; slightly raised processional ways were used for parades and for men and women to present sacrifices; deep 'lustral basins' for ritual washing *(katharsis)* are to be found in all palaces and the *polythyron*, a facade consisting of pillars and doors, which could be opened and closed to adjust the temperature, as in a conservatory.

Pottery

Kamares vases date from the Early Palatial Period, deriving their name from where they were found, the Kamares caves on the southern side of the Ida Mountains. The characteristic features are polychrome paintings on

Minoan ruins at Gournia and Phaistos

Kamares style vase

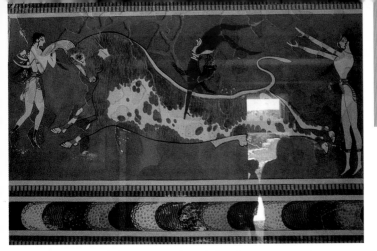

*Bull jumping fresco
from Knossos*

a dark background. Motifs from nature such as spirals and rosettes combine to create a harmonious unity.

Late Palatial Period vases of the so-called floral style display leaves or other plant motifs, while marine-style vessels are covered with octopus, paper nautilus or even coral designs. These vessels were either buried with the dead, given as votive offerings or else found in the palaces where they were in use as crockery.

Painting

Lilies, monkeys, partridges in a fantastic landscape and motifs from the natural world, these were the themes of Minoan artists. The paintings are purely two-dimensional, but with an impression of depth created by illustrations of landscape features around the four sides of the picture which draw on the main subject.

Pictures of imposing processions and rituals also feature as subjects. A procession of Minoan women with white skin and men with red skin is shown making a sacrificial offering. They carry sacred vessels with a hole in the base which is blocked by a hand until the sacrifice is offered. In a number of pictures, bare-breasted but otherwise magnificently dressed women sit or stand together in groups.

The mysteries of Minoan civilisation

Were the Minoan 'palaces' palaces at all? When the British archaeologist Arthur Evans uncovered the ruins of Knossos in 1900, he produced drawings that are now questioned by modern researchers.

Like the German archaeologist Heinrich Schliemann who discovered the ancient site of Troy, Evans was very familiar with the writings of Homer. The epic poet referred to King Minos, the wise ruler of Knossos who regularly

Ruins at Knossos

conferred with Zeus. Evans, therefore, assumed that the ruins at Knossos were the Palace of Minos and then proceeded to give names to the various rooms such as the 'King and Queen's Bedroom' and the 'Hall of the Double Axes'. The whole civilisation was 'Minoan'. But Homer lived in the 8th century BC, several hundred years after the demise of 'Minoan' civilisation. How can Evans be taken seriously? Perhaps the 'palaces' were just shrines, as the French archaeologist Paul Faure has suggested or even vast uninhabited palaces to the dead as Wunderlich, a German geologist, proposes. One clever solution to the mystery is to describe them as either 'palace temples' or 'temple palaces'.

However, a question that has never been answered satisfactorily is what precisely was the relationship between the theocrats at Knossos and their brethren in Malia, Phaistos and Zakros?

Also unclear is the role of women in Minoan civilisation. White-skinned women are shown in prominent positions on frescoes and seals, while smaller, red-skinned men are merely bystanders. None of the pictures show King Minos or any of his ancestors or successors. Archaeologists have been unable to provide any evidence of a king. The Minoan script known as Linear A or the ideograms on the Phaistos Disc which may shed some light on the structure of the state has not yet been deciphered. Was Minoan society matriarchal as some feminists have tried to show? It is probably safer to assume that women played a prominent role in the Minoan rituals at a time when a male-dominated society had not evolved.

Phaistos Disc

Venetian citadel at Rethymnon

Venetian fortresses

When the Venetians occupied Crete (13th–15th century), the principal foe lay in the east. The west was once again threatened by the infidel. In 1453, for the first time in history, what was thought to be an impregnable fortress fell victim to the Turkish military might: Constantinople. In the 16th century the Mediterranean was *mare turcicum*. By 1529 the Turks were within reach of Vienna. In 1522 they took the island of Rhodes, which had been in the hands of the Knights of St John. In 1571 Cyprus also fell into Ottoman hands. Christian victory at the Battle of Lepanto in the Gulf of Corinth in the same year did not stem the tide. At that time Crete was one of the last bastions of Christianity in the eastern Mediterranean. The Turks possessed the latest and most effective piece of military equipment, the cannon.

Medieval fortresses with machicolations, drawbridges and battlements were no longer capable of resisting determined armies. The Italian architect Michele Sanmicheli (1484–1559) had been charged with the task of modernising the Cretan fortresses in the towns of Heraklion, Rethymnon, and Chania and also the island fortresses at Gramvousa, Souda and Spinalonga.

The walls of these new fortifications were set at an angle in order to lessen the impact of cannonballs. An open slope (glacis) and a moat also helped to deter the enemy. Leaf-shaped bastions were built into the walls at intervals so that each section of wall could be protected. Sometimes a strongly built citadel was incorporated into the fortifications as at Rethymnon.

For the Italian architects of the Renaissance and those who commissioned them, a fortress was not just a purely functional building. It also had to fulfil certain aesthetic qualities which expressed the superiority of an urban civilisation. The star-shaped, strictly-controlled ground-plan was based on principles laid down by the polymath Alberti (1404–72), namely that a perfect state should also have perfect fortifications to protect it.

Byzantine church art

The finest examples of Byzantine art on Crete are to be found in the Panagia Kera near Kritsa, the church of the same name on the approach from Heraklion to the Lassithi Plain, and the monasteries at Gonia, Valsamonero and Toplou. The Icon Museum in St Catherine's Church at Heraklion also has some fine exhibits.

73

All stem from the time when Crete was under Venetian control. It is no surprise that Cretan art was influenced by the Venetians who also commissioned icons and churches. These differences led to conflict between the traditional style of painting, which tends towards orthodox canons of forms and content, and the westernised style

Cretan school icon

Panagia Kera Byzantine church

which adopted Italian form and content, e.g. naturalism, a sense of depth and perspective. This westernised artistic style is known as the 'Cretan School' with Michalis Damaskinos, El Greco's teacher, as its most important exponent. Six of his works are on show in the Icon Museum in Heraklion.

Churches are usually painted in the orthodox style, which can be further classified into a Vertical and Horizontal Hierarchy.

Vertical Hierarchy

Vertical Hierarchy: In the dome, or in the vaulting if there is no dome, Jesus, the *Pantokrator* (Almighty), looks down on the faithful. The Orthodox Church always emphasises the godly nature of Jesus with his mother Mary described as the *Theotokos* (Mother of God). In the drum of the dome, the next step down, the prophets and the archangels are portrayed holding spears. The 'heavenly host' stand in an almost military role by the side of Jesus, the king. In a socio-historic sense these celestial emissaries represent the Byzantine emperor. It should be remembered that the emperor was worshipped as a 'vicarious' authority, as the custodian of God's will on earth.

Further down the hierarchy come the four apostles, Matthew, Mark, Luke and John, in the Spherical Triangles, the section which bridges the circular dome and the nave. On the vaulting or on the walls are the Passion scenes, starting with the Annunciation on the south side of the church near the iconostasis and ending with the death of Mary on the north side. All Greek Orthodox churches have their altar on the east side. This Passion cycle is known as the Twelve Feast Cycle as it often focuses on the religious festivals of the year. It can, however, consist of more or less than twelve pictures. The lowest rung of the vertical hierarchy shows the saints, ascetics such as St Anthony, miracle healers like the holy *Paraskevi* or martyrs like St George. All are viewed from the front and look straight at the observer.

Horizontal Hierarchy: The most important part of the church is the altar in the sanctuary, where Mary is pictured above and the four Church Fathers below: John Chrysostomos (or the 'Golden Mouthed' on account of his oratorical skills), Gregory of Nazianzus, Basil the Great and Athanasius. Next comes the iconostasis, the illustrated screen, then the congregation and finally the exit with the portico or narthex at the west end. The Last Judgement with paradise or the torments of hell is depicted above the exit or in the narthex. It is placed here to remind the faithful before they leave the church what can happen should they fail to comply with the teachings and demands of church and state.

Modern Cretan Culture

Songs of love and suffering

Mantinades and rizitika, music and dancing

Mantinades and rizitika comprise rhyming couplets which are sung to the accompaniment of the *lyra* (played with a bow) and a *laouto* (plucked). The songs are about love and suffering, about war and everyday worries and cares and are sung at christenings and marriages, at religious festivals – or simply after an enjoyable family meal. In wedding songs, the bridegroom likes to be portrayed as an eagle – the highest compliment that can be paid in a patriarchal society such as Crete, as the eagle is bold, strong and brave. The bride, on the other hand, is a partridge, small and pretty, but not very mobile – partridges can only fly a few hundred yards at a time.

Cretans dance in groups

When the guests have finished eating – probably not until 11pm – the *lyra* and *laouto* players will start up and the dancing will commence. Cretan dancing is not couples together but several men and women standing in closed or open rounds with either shoulders or hands touching. There are three basic dances: *pentozalis*, *chaniotikos* and *sousta*. Probably the most rousing of the three is the *sousta*. Here only the lower part of the body moves while the shoulders stay in a straight line.

Where is it possible to see Cretan dancing? It might be difficult to join in private family celebrations so two options can be considered. First study the calendar of religious festivals (*see page 77*) or visit one of the *kritika kentra*, the large music bars which exist in the bigger towns. Usually only open on Friday and Saturday, these are popular with the locals.

Literature

By far the most famous modern Greek writer is the Cretan Nikos Kazantzakis (1883–1957). As a child he experienced the uprisings against the Turks as his father was active within the resistance movement. His experiences in the War of Independence and his religious background play an important part in his later books. Even as a young man Kazantzakis was well aware of the narrow perspectives of Greek Orthodoxy. He studied Buddhism and the Roman Catholic faith. Francis of Assisi, the son of wealthy parents who renounced money and property and dedicated his life to the poor, was his role model. El Greco, who looked beyond the shores of Crete but never denied his origins also influenced his thinking. He revered men of action such as Lenin and Alexis Zorba. Kazantzakis' major literary contribution was *Zorba the Greek* (1946) and *Freedom or Death* (1953). *Report to El Greco*, an autobiography, was written shortly before his death in 1957 and many regard it as his best work.

'Zorba the Greek' Village

Kazantzakis' writings, especially certain passages in *Freedom or Death* and many parts of his later novel *The Last Temptation of Christ*, brought him into conflict with the church and almost resulted in his excommunication. In the face of uproar from the literary world, however, it was decided simply to put both books on the Index – the Vatican's list of forbidden books. In 1955, Kazantzakis was nominated for the Nobel Prize for Literature, but the church managed to prevent this honour being bestowed upon him.

Another Cretan writer was Pandelis Prevelakis, a contemporary of Kazantzakis. His books deal with the Turkish wars and the bravery of the Cretans.

Zorba's Dance

The film *Zorba the Greek* brought international fame to Kazantzakis. It tells of a how a bookworm who would much rather read about love than fall in love himself meets Zorba, a man who cannot read or write but can dance and seduce women, and accepts things as they are. Together they establish themselves as men of action and both form sensitive relationships with women.

Anthony Quinn in Zorba the Greek

Michalis Cacoyannis, the Hollywood producer of Cypriot origin, made the film in 1964. Anthony Quinn took the leading role as Zorba with Alan Bates as the bookworm and Irini Papas as an attractive widow. The famous *sirtaki* dance caused a number of problems for the islanders as it is not a genuine Cretan dance at all. It proved too difficult for the American actor to learn so composer Theodorakis came up with a simple but haunting melody in its place. The hordes of tourists who later came to Crete asked to see a dance which did not actually exist, but hoteliers and the music industry moved quickly to fill the gap. At today's 'Cretan evenings' *sirtaki* is performed and cassettes of the catchy tune are available everywhere.

Festivals and Folklore

A Minoan murals depicts a harvest festival, with the people gathered in the courtyard, the women dressed in their best and their dark hair elaborately styled. The priestess is about to give the sign for the tournament to begin, and seven young men and women are to perform a breakneck leap over the bull. Later the people might go outside until the evening and then reassemble in the theatre to watch the dance of the girls.

Just like their forebears, the Cretans like nothing more than a good celebration. Any excuse will do. Most festivals today are in honour of the saints, and on their name days, a service is held in the church dedicated to the saint, which is followed by a public festival. In the case of religious festivals, the dancing and *lyra* music celebrations usually take place on the eve of the saint's day.

40 days before Easter: Carnival *(Apokries)* takes place in the two weeks preceding Lent and is an excuse for costume parties and high spirits.

Clean Monday *(Kathari Deftera)* is the first day of Lent in the Orthodox calendar. Cretan skies are filled with kites.

Easter Week: The *Epitaphios* procession, a funeral procession with a flower-bedecked bier, passes through the streets on Good Friday evening, but by midnight on Saturday the mood has changed considerably. The priest calls *Christos anesti* (Christ is risen) and lights his candle from the Holy Flame in the sanctuary. Those standing nearby

Preparing for Easter

Cathedral of Agios Minas

light their candle from his flame, the light is passed on to the rest of the congregation and so begins the candlelit procession. Outside the church a funeral pyre is lit and Judas symbolically perishes in the flames. Candle in hand everyone returns home but the light must not be extinguished. After midnight the fast is broken with a special Easter soup called *Margiritsa* which is made from lamb's liver and entrails, egg, lemon and rice. On Easter Sunday, the paschal lamb is roasted on a spit and houses are decked with lilac.

Liver soup

Greek Orthodox Easter is a movable feast and rarely coincides with the Protestant and Catholic Easter.

Easter dates for the rest of the decade are as follows: 14 April 1996; 27 April 1997, 19 April 1998; 11 April 1999.

Water melons have their own special day

March	**25** Independence Day and the Annunciation. Military parades and procession of schoolchildren.
April	Snail festival in Vamos
	23 St George's day celebrated at the churches of St George. If this date falls during the period of fasting, then it is moved to Easter Monday.
May	**1** Labour Day and the beginning of summer. Garlands are hung on doors and barbecues lit outside.
	20–27 In Chania the Battle of Crete in 1941 is remembered.
June	Wine festival in the village of Gerakari near Rethymnon.
	24 Bonfires are lit all over Greece to celebrate the summer solstice and the birth of John the Baptist. The custom is to jump over the fire, though usually only young boys do this.
July	Wine festival in Rethymnon, Heraklion and Dafnes.
	27 Water melon festival in Chersonisos.
July/August	Concerts and plays in Heraklion.
	Cretan evenings in the village of Gavalochori east of Chania.
	Renaissance festival in Rethymnon.
	Lato festival in Agios Nikolaos.
	Festival of Culture in Sitia.
August	**5–6** Procession at Archanes to celebrate the Transfiguration of Christ *(Jouchtas)*. Wine festival in Kastelli, near Heraklion.
	10–15 *Lyra* music festival in Anogia.
	15 Assumption Day is celebrated in many towns and villages, churches and monasteries of St Mary. The Chrisoskalitisa fes-

Chrisoskalitisa Monastery

tival at in western Crete is particularly colourful, with dancing and *lyra* music.

15–18 Wine festival in Sitia.

Festival of political songs in Vamos.

Second half of August: three-day folk festival in Kritsa.

25 Large procession in Heraklion and Gortyn in honour of St Titus, Crete's patron saint.

End of August: Grape festival in Perama near Rethymnon.

31 Feast of St Alexander on Lassithi Plain.

September **Beginning of September**: Day of the Fisherman in Rethymnon.

14 Erection of cross on Timios Stavros (Psiloritis) in the Ida Mountains.

14 Grape festival on the Thripti Plateau.

Festival of tourism at Rethymnon.

Tourists at Rethymnon

October White cabbage festival in Agia Varvara near Heraklion.

Psarovradia (Fisherman's Evening) in Elounda near Agios Nikolaos.

Chestnut festival in Elos.

28 *Ochi* (No) Day. On this day in 1940, Greece defied the Italian surrender ultimatum.

79

November **7–9** Anniversary of the 1866 explosion at Arkadi Monastery remembered in Rethymnon.

11 Feast of St Minas, Heraklion's patron saint.

Rethymnon's fishermen celebrate in September

Food and Drink

The ingredients for Greek food do not have to travel very far to get to the table. There is a difference between cooked dishes (meals served straight from the saucepan) and meals which are prepared 'while you wait' *(tis oras)* where a little more time is required. Similarly, there are two types of restaurants: the *estiatorion* serves dishes from the hot plate, whereas a *taverna* serves freshly grilled meat or fish. Another kind of *taverna* is the *psarotaverna*, a fish *taverna*. A *magirion* is a variation of the *estiatorion*. Literally translated it means 'lunch table'.

The *estiatorion* is only for eating, a *taverna* on the other hand is open in the evenings as a place to relax. These are the traditional differences but nowadays the line is blurring and, of course, other types of restaurants are appearing, such as *pizzerias*, snack bars and also foreign – French, German, Chinese and Indian – restaurants. In some resorts there are even vegetarian and wholefood restaurants.

How to choose the right restaurant

Greek restaurants are officially classified into various categories. Top-class restaurants will provide a clean tablecloth for every new customer, butter and candles will be on the table and perhaps fishing nets will hang from the ceiling, whereas at others there will be harsh neon lighting and re-usable plastic plates to eat from. However, the official category of a restaurant says nothing about the quality of the food, only about the setting. Of course, Greek restaurateurs know that there is easy money to be earned from tourists. Complaints by tourists about 'too much olive oil' have come at the right time for cooks trying to save on expensive ingredients. Now olive oil is either diluted with sunflower oil from EU surpluses or omitted altogether. Other tourists grumble about frozen food, tinned peas or caterers' factory-prepared chips, when in fact that is all they ever eat at home. And yet the Greeks would turn up their noses if they were served such 'Euro' fare.

One way to judge whether a restaurant really cares about its customers is to find one that opens all year round. Such restaurants have to depend on their Greek customers, not tourists. If the bread is fresh, if there is sufficient salad for two people, it is dressed with pure olive oil and there is no rice and potato mixture as a side dish to the *souvlaki*, then you have chosen the right place to eat.

And where to drink

As well as places to eat there are *ouzeria* where *ouzo* and *raki* are drunk with *mezedes*, typically Greek (but also very Middle Eastern) snacks and nibbles. A variety of *mezedes* on one plate are called *pikilia* or 'colourful plate'.

A light lunch

Coffee time

A good choice of cheese

Traditionally, restaurants are not cafés in the true sense of the word. Coffee and cakes are available from the *zacharoplastion*, the *galaktopolion* serves milk products and the *kafenion* just coffee and other drinks but nothing to eat.

Cretan specialities

Cretan fare differs little from what is eaten in the rest of Greece. Admittedly, every region has its own specialities, but these only mean minor changes to the Greek menu.

What is special about Cretan food? There are a number of different types of cheese. *Anthotiro*, for example, is a soft creamy cheese and tastes a little saltier than *mizithra* but not as salty as *feta* cheese. *Kefalotiri*, on the other hand, is hard and crumbly. Both sorts of cheese are rich in protein and are not cheap. They are produced in the mountains by sheep and goat farmers. To accompany their cheese the farmers, who may live miles from the nearest baker, will eat *paximadi,* dark rusks. These resemble large, flat stones and will remain very hard until they are dipped in water or milk just prior to eating. Some Cretans break them up and add them to the salad dressings.

Mountain tea is a favourite non-alcoholic drink. *Malotira* and *diktamus* are supposed to provide relief from practically all complaints. *Malotira* is a Venetian word comprising *male* and *tirare* and meaning roughly 'that which draws out evil'. *Diktamus* or dittany is still valued for its aphrodisiac qualities.

Raki is the local 'firewater'. It is a stronger version of *ouzo* and, for Cretan menfolk, how much *raki* can be consumed in one session is still a test of virility. It is also regarded as something of a panacea, particularly in the villages. *Raki* is served as a welcoming drink for guests and even the poorest families will keep a bottle in the house

A family gathering

for unexpected visitors. Hotel bars in the tourist resorts will not normally serve it to guests. It is intended for household use and not for sale.

Cretan red wines will taste different from one village to the next. Only bar owners retain the old tradition and serve it straight from the barrel – the profit margin on bottled wine is much greater.

Retsina, Greece's resinated wine, is in fact not as popular on Crete as on the mainland. For many the resinous flavour of the wine is too prominent anyway, in which case *aretsinoto* (unresinated) may be more acceptable.

Two reliable brands of wine sold on Crete are Gortinos and Clos du Castel. Minos produces the best rosé on the island and their red and white wines are also quite drinkable.

Local wines for sale

Cretan bananas

Banana plantations can be seen in the hotter eastern and southern parts of Crete. To speed up the ripening process, the farmers wrap plastic bags around the 'hands'. The resulting fruit is smaller than their counterparts from central America, but they are tastier although relatively expensive. Until recently, the Greek government protected Greek banana production from competition. The importation of Caribbean and South American bananas was banned but the demand for Greek bananas was such that dealers were able to take advantage of the prices fixed by the government. Cretan bananas disappeared from the market stalls and were sold under the counter at exhorbitant prices. Only after the market was opened up to foreign competition did the price stabilise at normal levels.

83

Italian alternative

Restaurant selection

In the following selection, $$$ = expensive; $$ = medium priced; $ = cheap.

Agia Galini: Discos, bars and breakfast cafés galore. The only traditional *kafenion* here is **Synantesis** which is situated on the middle lane through to the harbour.

Agios Nikolaos: Most restaurants are geared towards tourist meals with little attempt to provide Cretan fare. **$Haris** by the harbour has an authentic feel and is favoured by the locals. **$$$Ariadne** also by the harbour serves upmarket Cretan dishes.

Archanes: Kostas garden *taverna* opposite the village church. The owner will help to locate the site attendants.

Arkadi Monastery: There is a shop and self-service restaurant in front of the monastery.

Chania: Aeriko, about 200m east of the old town by the sea, serves superb *mezedes*. Some good fish restaurants in Nea Chora by the fishing port. **$Africana** is a family-run concern at the end of the beach. Some restaurants occupy the cellars of Venetian and Turkish houses in the old town. **$Tamam**, for example, is in an old Turkish bathhouse (Zambeliou 49) and **$Pafsilon** is hidden away near Platia Venizelou. **$Vassilis** in the same square is probably the last remaining traditional *kafenion* in the district although, as a gesture to the 20th century, cocktails are included on the menu.

Chersonisos: $$Taverna Pharos is on the cape by the fishing port. It offers good *mezedes* and a sea view.

Elounda: Good fish restaurants around the harbour. On Spinalonga an old-fashioned *taverna* whose electricity is supplied by generator stands near the windmills and an early Christian mosaic.

Georgioupolis: $Arkadi enjoys a good position. Near the river mouth by the sea. Cross the bridge and then follow the west coast of the river. **$Jorgo's Tavern** serves good food. By the main road on the edge of town.

Eating out in Heraklion

Heraklion: *Tavernas* are to be found everywhere in the old town, but mainly near the Lion Fountain and in the market quarter. A number of very reasonably-priced restaurants with a good atmosphere are to be found in Odhos Karterou, the narrow lane that links the market street and Odhos Evans. Try Daskalogiannis Square for other good value *ouzerias* and restaurants. **$$$Kyriakos** at Demokratias 45 (the road out towards Knossos) serves upmarket Greek fare.

Ierapetra: $$Gorgona near the fortress has a very good reputation.

Imbros Gorge: Two *tavernas* on the asphalt road round the bend to the right. Taxis can be ordered here for the return journey.

An abundance of fresh fish

Kastelli Kissamou: The *tavernas* on the narrow promenade serve good food, but **$$Psaria** by the fishing port is the best place to eat. Freshly caught fish is not kept for days in the refrigerator here, but goes straight from the fishing boat to the kitchen to the plate.

Kokkino Chorio: There are a few *kafenia* in Kokkino Chorio and a *taverna* in Plaka. Wine is served straight from the barrel.

Malia: Like Chersonisos, the restaurants here generally offer below average quality meals at above average prices. **$$Malia Port** fish *taverna* by the harbour is one of the better establishments. The *tavernas* around the *platia* in the centre of the village are cheaper. Draught country wines are often served here. It is probably worth looking further afield to restaurants at Sissi and Milatos (10km/6 miles and 20km/12 miles respectively). The **$$Latsida** restaurant at the National Highway service station by the tunnel between Malia and Agios Nikolaos serves surprisingly good meals with *souvlaki* a speciality.

Margarites: The restaurant beneath the branches of a mulberry tree in the *platia* is a relaxing place to eat. Diners can also enjoy a fine view down to the coast.

Matala: **$$The Two Brothers of Matala** is an old-fashioned restaurant on the *platia*. The beach restaurants specialise mainly in fish, but there is not enough fresh fish to meet the demand. Ask for *fresko psari* when ordering and not *katapsigmeno psari* (frozen fish).

Palaeochora: Most breakfast cafés serve muesli – Palaeochora has a health-conscious clientele. **$$Savvas** by the town hall is a traditional establishment, but the restaurant near the health centre also has a good reputation.

Plakias: **$Taverna Loukas** near the bridge serves very good quality food, including fresh fish. Other *tavernas* by the beaches east and west of the town.

Rethymnon: A candlelit meal in a fish *taverna* by the romantic Venetian harbour is an essential part of a visit to Rethymnon. However, the *tavernas* in the old town are less crowded and offer better meals. Dancing and *lyra* music accompanies diners in **$$Gounakis**, Koroneou 8.

Rodia: **$Taverna Iremvi** at the entrance to Rodia serves excellent Cretan fare at very reasonable prices. Panorama.

Sitia: Traditional *estiatorion* at Kornarou 27. **$Sorbas** by the harbour, Platia K. Zotou has a good choice of dishes.

Spili: Plenty of good, cheap *tavernas* around the *platia*.

Vai: There are several establishments to take care of the needs of the many visitors.

Zaros: Several fish *tavernas* which serve fresh trout and salmon. Zaros is the only place in Crete where fresh-water fish are farmed.

Taverna menu

Salad assortment

Vai has it all

85

Shopping

Hand-woven blankets are a speciality

Pottery has a long tradition

Cretan doll

Take home some olives

Cretan tourist resorts are full of souvenir shops selling over-priced kitsch and junk. However, if you can manage to steer clear of these places, there are some genuine treasures to be had. These include hand-woven blankets, embroidery work, metal and wood crafts, ceramics and earthenware, as well as spices and herbal teas – all of which have been important export commodities as far back as Minoan times.

Crete, and above all Chania, is famous for its leather goods, including bags, sandals and especially boots of cowhide imported from Africa. Unglazed ceramic storage jars of the kind produced on Crete 4,000 years ago (used mainly as flower pots today), plus other pots and jugs of all sizes are sold along the roads just outside towns. Hand-woven, hand-embroidered or crocheted blankets and fabrics are still important products of the native crafts industry, although industrial copies are stepping up the competition. The women of Kritsa and Anogia produce hand-woven fabrics and embroidery of a particularly high standard.

Market vendors and small household goods shops sell wicker baskets, as well as wooden spoons and the traditional *brikia* – the small copper coffeepots with long handles used to make Greek coffee. Brass coffee grinders are widely available and most china stores will stock the tiny, white *kafenion* cups.

Cretan knives, originally part of the traditional costume, are long and curved with thick white handles and silver scabbards. The old ones are rare and expensive, but they also come in various shapes and sizes as souvenirs. A whole range of other knives are also available, from chopping knives to the curved knives used to prune grapevines.

Gold and silver are relatively inexpensive in Crete and Greece generally – which explains the abundance of jewellery shops, often selling machine-made merchandise.

There are a number of culinary delights worth bringing home, including the sharp, firm cheese called *graviera*; honey (*meli*), especially the thyme-scented variety; black and green olives in brine; and *tsikouthia*, Crete's version of *raki*. The local marketplace is the place to go for most of these items – here you'll also find a whole array of herbs and spices, from *rigani* (oregano) to Cretan saffron and spicy cinnamon bark. You can also take the opportunity to stock up on *passatempo* from any street cart – paper bags full of peanuts, pistachios, roasted chickpeas, pumpkin seeds, etc.

EOMMECH is the state-run handicraft centre. In Heraklion it is situated in Zografou (also houses an exhibition of work by local artisans); in Chania it is in Venizelou 4.

Nightlife

Bars, discos and clubs abound in the holiday resorts, but there is nothing distinctively Greek about them, in fact in most cases you feel you could be just about anywhere. Resort hotels often lay on evenings of 'authentic traditional entertainment' which includes music, dancing and even costumes – the only thing missing are the Cretans themselves. The *kritika kentra*, traditional nightclubs located on the outskirts of town or even further out in the country, are used for weddings as well as evenings of live Cretan music. People also come here to eat and drink, but mainly to dance Cretan dances. The *skilathika* are similar but sleazier clubs imported from the mainland, their dance music furnished by second- or third-rate *bouzouki* ensembles. A *skilathiko* is the final stop of many a late-evening tour of the nightspots, and is one of the few places where you're at all likely to see Greeks drinking heavily (whisky is sold by the bottle at grossly inflated prices).

Heraklion: Live *lyra* music is on offer at several *kritika kentra*, such as the **Kastro** on Beaufort above the harbour. **Palazzo Itar** and **Veneto** in Epimenidou are friendly bars housed in old Venetian villas. There are also a number of discos nearby. The area around the Lion Fountain offers the widest choice of bars.

Chania: Discos and bars abound behind the Mosque of the Janissaries and by the yacht marina. *Lyra* music can be heard at *kritika kentra* outside the town in Mournies, for example. Also outside the town in Agia is the unusual **Tutti Frutti**, a disco with garden and swimming pool.

Palaeochora: Palaeochora Club by the campsite has an open-air disco. Several cocktail bars by the beach.

The night is yet young

Night lights

87

The youth of Crete

Active Holidays

Crete offers all kinds of sporting possibilities from swimming, snorkelling, windsurfing and sailing to hiking, climbing and even skiing.

Walking and mountain climbing

The best maps for walking in Crete are produced by Harms Verlág – there are five in their 1:80,000 series, covering the island from west to east.

The old bridlepaths, a network of tracks that cover the whole island, are ideal for walkers. Several travel companies offer organised walking holidays on the island. On Crete itself contact the Mountain Climbing Bureau with branches in Rethymnon (A. Sikelianou 10, tel: (0831) 21355 and Chania (K. Dimitriou, on Platia Venizelou by the harbour, tel: (0821) 44946. The Hellenic Alpine Club (EOS) is run by amateurs and organises walks for the local people. For further information contact the following private numbers: Heraklion, tel: (081) 227609. Rethymnon, tel: (0831) 22710. Chania, tel: (0821) 24647. Guides and equipment are also available for climbers wishing to scale the heights of the Ida Mountains or peaks in the White Mountains.

Apart from the Samaria Gorge, the Imbros and Rouvas gorges make good walks. The White Mountains (Lefka Ori) are a wild and unspoilt region with Pachnes at 2,452m (8,042ft) their highest peak. Inexperienced walkers should take care as it is easy to get lost on the heights. There are no maps available which show the paths that link the villages at the foot of the mountain with the shepherds' cheese production plants on the upper hillsides. Another difficulty arises from the similarity in appearance of the various cone-shaped summits. Water can only be obtained from the shepherds' tanks and snow covers the mountains until well into June.

The Ida Mountains (Oros Idi) are less dangerous even though one of the peaks, Psiloritis (2,456m/8,055ft), is the highest mountain on Crete. It can be climbed in one day. An easier route for walkers branches off to the left of the metalled road between Anogia and Nida Plain. It takes three hours to reach the entrance to the Rouvas Gorge and then after another two hours, the Zaros country park, where a *taverna* with a lakeside garden offers refreshment.

Skiing

This is also possible in Crete during the winter months – though don't expect any resorts resembling Val d'Isère or Chamonix, or you're bound to be disappointed. For more information contact the Haniá branch of the Hellenic Alpine Club (*see above*).

Watersports

Crete is a watersport enthusiast's paradise. Opportunities for windsurfing, water-skiing and paragliding are available in all the main resorts and at many beaches. The seawater off the Cretan beaches is reckoned to be among the cleanest in Europe. There is a new windsurfing centre in Plaka near Elounda, while divers can choose between The Divers in Plakias, the Barracuda Club and the Crete Watersports Centre in Agia Pelagia or Overschmidt International in the Grecotels in Gouves and near Rethymnon (Rethimna Beach Hotel).

Fishing enthusiasts require no special licence, but underwater spear fishing is restricted. Seabass, swordfish and dentex are the most common catch.

On account of the many underwater archaeological sites around the island, scuba diving is restricted to designated areas. Snorkelling is permitted everywhere, however, and it can be quite a rewarding pursuit, especially around Mirabello Bay, where from Elounda Beach you can swim out to see the sunken Greco-Roman city of Olous.

Unfortunately, the cleanliness of the water does not match the cleanliness of the beaches. During the winter months plastic rubbish and lumps of crude oil are often deposited on the beaches. Thankfully, the districts where tourism is a major source of income ensure that at the beginning of the season the sand is 'ploughed' and the rubbish collected.

Cycle tours and mountain biking

There are steep hills, quiet country roads and farm tracks in abundance. The Cretan Mountain Climbing Bureau organises cycle tours, as does Hellas Bike Travel which is based at the Rethimna Beach Hotel. Cycles can be hired in most coastal resorts.

Fishing at Lefkogia beach

Windsurfing

89

Mountain bikes for hire

Getting There

By air

There are three ways to get to Crete by air:

1 Direct charter flight to Crete, arriving in Heraklion or Chania
2 Scheduled flight to Athens, then connecting flight to Crete
3 Scheduled or charter flight to Athens, then ferry to Crete

Opposite: welcome to Crete

Happy landings

New arrivals

There are no international scheduled flights direct to Crete so most visitors arrive on charter flights either as part of a package holiday or on a flight-only deal. Direct charters are to Heraklion and less frequently to Chania; they depart from regional airports in the UK (flight time: 4 hours), as well as from Ireland and other European cities (no direct flights from the US).

All scheduled flights involve changing planes in Athens. For airlines apart from Olympic Airways, this means changing terminals, too. Olympic Airways, the main carrier, operates direct flights from Britain (London, Heathrow) and from the US (New York) to Athens. The airline also runs up to eight scheduled flights daily from Athens to Heraklion (flight time: 50 minutes) and from six flights daily to Chania (flight time: 45 minutes).

Olympic Airways in the UK:
11 Conduit Street, London W1R OLP
Tel: (0171) 409 2400.
In the US:
645 Fifth Avenue, New York 10022
Tel: (212) 838 3600.

Buses from the Heraklion airport only go to Heraklion. The blue city buses run every 20 minutes to the Platia Eleftherias in the centre and then to the western suburbs via Chanion Porta (bus station for the Messara Plain). Tickets must be bought at special kiosks situated by the main bus-stops and at the airport. For other destinations, take a taxi. A board at the airport exit gives distances to main destinations and approximate fares.

There are no service buses from the Chania airport to Chania. Passengers with Olympic Airways can pick up a bus at the town's office, Tzanakaki 88.

Buy your tickets before you board

By sea

Bear in mind that ferry schedules change frequently, especially between the summer and winter seasons. The best place to gain up-to-date information is from the Greek tourist office (*see page 95*), or from any travel agent in Greece (the latter also sell ferry tickets).

Island ferry

From the Greek mainland: ANEK and Minoan shipping lines operate daily car and passenger ferry services from Piraeus to Heraklion and Chania (Souda Bay). Both trips take approximately 12 hours and run through the night, leaving Piraeus in the early evening (berths and cabins available). Another company, Rethimniaki, offers a service (four ferries a week) from Piraeus to Rethymnon. Ferries also run between the Peloponnese and the island of Kithira, from where there are connecting services to Kastelli in western Crete.

From other Greek islands: There are frequent ferries from many of the Cycladic islands (daily from Santorini/Thira). A regular ferry service also operates from Rhodes to Agios Nikolaos, Sitia and Heraklion.

From Italy: Ferries run regularly from Brindisi, Ancona, Bari and Otranto in Italy via the Greek island of Corfu to Patra and Igoumenitsa on the Greek mainland. Two shipping lines, Adriatica and Marlines, offer a direct service from Italy to Crete in July and August – the former runs from Venice to Heraklion and the latter from Ancona to Patra and Heraklion

By rail
The main rail route from London to Athens takes around three and a half days, travelling down through France and Italy, and crossing over to Greece by ferry from the Adriatic port of Brindisi.

By car
Taking a car on to the island of Crete can be an expensive business, and car hire should be considered as an alternative. The main route from London to Athens is through France and Italy, a distance of approximately 2,400 km/1,500 miles (not including the ferry crossing from Italy to Greece). The route via the former Yugoslavia is possible but it is no longer recommended: ask your local motoring organisation before setting out. Otherwise, for those determined to travel overland all the way to Greece, the best alternative route is via France, Belgium, Germany, Austria, Hungary, Romania and Bulgaria, arriving over the border in northeast Greece.

Before setting out consult the Greek tourist office or a motoring organisation such as the AA for advice on insurance requirements and any special regulations for countries en route. A national driving licence, vehicle registration documents and third-party insurance are all compulsory – though comprehensive cover is strongly recommended. If you are passing through any non-EU countries, an international driving permit and green insurance card will also be required (otherwise your cover will be third party only).

Getting Around

No shortage of taxis

By bus

You can rely on KTEL

Two companies share the island's overland services: KTEL Heraklion/Lassithi and KTEL Rethymnon/Chania, whose buses are modern, reliable and inexpensive. Each major town has its own bus terminal (or terminals). Timetables (also available in English) can be obtained there, as well as at travel agencies, tourist information offices and the airport. Buses run approximately every hour between the major towns, whereas in the outlying villages, there will probably be two buses per day, one in the morning and one in the afternoon.

From Heraklion, buses for southern Crete and the Messara Plain, Anogia, Rodia and Fodele leave from the Chanion Porta bus station just outside the fortifications. Rethymnon/Chania and Agios Nikolaos/Sitia are served from the harbour bus station about 200m east of the old Venetian harbour.

Taxis

Taxi fares are controlled by the government. In some instances, four people can travel more cheaply together in a taxi than by bus. It is not worth trying to negotiate a fare in advance. It will not be less than the metered fare. Village taxis, marked *agoraion,* do not have meters, but the tariffs are fixed and one taxi will be no cheaper than another.

Apart from the cost, an advantage of taking a taxi is the driver's knowledge of the area. It is usually possible to arrange for the driver to drop you off somewhere and pick you up a few hours later, or alternatively, you can negotiate a private sightseeing tour.

Note that a tip of about 10 percent is customary, but not obligatory, for taxi-drivers.

By car

Driving is on the right in Greece and road signs follow standard European conventions, though on country byways you may come across some signs in Greek only. Despite the fact that there is a good network of roads on the island, visitors should be aware that the Cretan style of driving takes some getting used to – on highways motorists pass on the right or left without warning and frequently use the hard shoulder as an extra lane; in villages red lights are commonly viewed as a suggestion rather than a rule.

High speeds are not recommended – there are too many unexpected hazards, whether it be a paved road that suddenly becomes a dirt track without warning, a huge pothole or rock in the middle of the road, or an entire herd of sheep appearing out of nowhere. The speed limit on national highways is 100 kph (62 mph) for cars and 70 kph (44 mph) for motorbikes; on country roads it is 70 kph and in towns 50 kph (31 mph).

Although usually ignored, the use of seatbelts in cars is required by law, as are helmets for motorcyclists. Should you break down or require emergency road assistance while driving on the island, the number to ring is 174. The **Automobile and Touring Club of Greece (ELPA)** will also help members of affiliated motoring organisations such as the AA or RAC. Their numbers are as follows – Heraklion: (081) 289440; Rethymnon: (0831) 20554; Chania: (0821) 26059; Agios Nikolaos: (0841) 22620.

Car hire

There are scores of car rental agencies on the island offering the normal range of hire cars as well as four-wheel-drive vehicles. International companies such as Avis and Hertz are considerably more expensive than their local counterparts, who are generally just as reliable. Whoever you rent from, be sure to check carefully the insurance being offered – full coverage is strongly recommended – and whether it is included in the price quoted. Payment by credit card is usually preferred. You will need to produce an international driving permit or a valid national licence that has been held for at least one year (a passport is also sometimes requested). The minimum age for renting a car in Crete varies from 18 to 21, depending on the agency.

Motorbikes for hire

Bicycle and motorbike hire

Motorbikes, mopeds and bicycles are widely available in all the resort towns. Mopeds are ideal for short distances on reasonably flat terrain, but the interior is too mountainous for anything but a motorbike. Make sure, whatever you hire, that the vehicle is in good condition and that the price includes proper insurance. Be sure too to wear a helmet.

Facts for the Visitor

Travel documents

Visitors from EU countries (including Britain and Eire), Canada, the US, Australia and New Zealand need only a valid passport and can stay for a period of up to three months. For longer stays a resident's permit must be obtained from the local police in Crete.

Customs

Visitors from EU countries may bring the following goods duty-free into Greece (note that the same quantities apply to duty-paid goods from outside the EU): 200 cigarettes or 100 cigarillos or 50 cigars or 250 g tobacco (18 years or over); 2 litres wine or 1 litre spirits or 2 litres liqueurs (18 years or over); 60 ml perfume; 250 ml eau de toilette. Allowances for duty-paid goods from within the EU are significantly more generous.

Note that the export of antiquities and archaeological artefacts from Greece is strictly prohibited.

Tourist information

The National Tourist Organisation of Greece (*Ellinikos Organismos Tourismou* or EOT) maintains offices in most European capitals, North America and Australia. They will provide free of charge maps and brochures on Crete (in English), bus and ferry schedules, opening times of museums and archaeological sites, as well as hotel listings.

In the UK: 4 Conduit Street London W1R 0DJ, tel: (0171) 734 5997, fax: (0171) 287 1369.

In the US: Olympic Tower, 645 Fifth Avenue, New York, NY 10022, tel: 421 5777, fax: 826 6940; 611 West Sixth Street, Suite 2198, Los Angeles, California 90017, tel: 626 6696, fax: 489 9744; 168 North Michigan Avenue, Chicago, Illinois 60601, tel: 782 1084, fax 782 1091.

EOT on Crete: Heraklion – opposite the Archaeological Museum, tel: (081) 228225 or (081) 226081 or (081) 228203, fax: (081) 226020; **Agios Nikolaos** – by Lake Voulismeni, tel: (0841) 22357; **Rethymnon** – on the promenade, tel: (0831) 29148; **Chania** – in Kriari 40, tel: (0821) 92624

Currency and exchange

The Greek unit of currency is the drachma (*drahmi* in Greek; plural *drahmes*). The most common denominations are notes worth 50, 100, 500, 1,000 and 5,000 drachmas and coins of 5, 10, 20 and 50 drachmas. You are officially allowed to bring into Greece no more than 100,000 drachmas, though any amount of foreign currency and travellers' cheques may be imported. Anything over

Beach life at Matala

95

Holiday images

There are banks in all major towns and resorts

US$1,000 (or equivalent) should be declared on entry, in case this money needs to be exported again.

There are banks in all major towns and resorts, but be prepared for long queues. Exchange facilities are also available at post offices (which often offer a better rate than the banks), travel agents, hotels and tourist offices. Always take your passport with you when exchanging money or cashing travellers' cheques, and check the rates and commission charges beforehand, as they vary considerably. In the main towns, local currency can also be withdrawn on a credit card at most cashpoint machines.

Eurocheques are accepted by banks and post offices but not shops, while major credit cards are accepted by the more expensive shops, hotels and restaurants, as well as all car rental agencies.

Tipping
Waiters usually expect a tip of about 10 percent, as do other service personnel.

Opening times
Business hours: Monday, Wednesday, Saturday: about 8am–2pm, Tuesday, Thursday, Friday: about 8am–1pm and 5–8.30pm.

Banks are open from 8am to 2pm, while post offices open earlier and close later, ie 7.30am–2 or 3pm, in the main towns until 6pm.

The OTE, the Greek telecommunications company, does not have fixed opening times, but in the main towns their offices are open all day and often well into the evening.

Museums and archaeological sights are usually open from 8.30am to 3pm but are closed on Monday. The major sites such as Knossos, Phaistos, Malia and Heraklion Archaeological Museum have longer opening hours and also stay open on Monday.

Icons for sale

Souvenirs
Leather goods, weaving, pottery from Thrapsano and Margarites, embroidery and crocheted shawls always make good souvenirs or presents. EOMMECH (*see also page 86*) is a state-run organisation for craftsmen and artisans, with branches in Chania and Heraklion. The staff here will provide addresses of studios and exhibitions where craft work is on display.

Honey and olive oil, said to be the best in Europe, are always appreciated at home, unlike Cretan wine which does not travel well.

Public holidays
1 January, 25 March (Independence Day), Good Friday (until noon), Easter Sunday, 1 May, 25 December. On these

days Museums, archaeological sites and businesses are usually closed.

Postal services

Postboxes are bright yellow and, if there are two slots to choose from, *esoteriko* means inland and *exoteriko* means overseas. Post offices (*tachydromeia*) and are also easily recognisable by their bright yellow signs with blue writing – the main branches will usually change money in addition to handling mail, but long-distance phone calls must be made from an OTE office (*see below*). Stamps (*grammatosima*) can be purchased at any post office or *periptero* (kiosk).

The post office sign

Telephone

Postal services and the telephone network are not linked and it is not possible to phone from post offices. Cheap-rate calls start at 10pm.

In many towns the Greek telephone company OTE has offices with phone booths. Many public phones are now card-operated and cards from 1,000 Dr. may be obtained from kiosks. Long-distance calls can be made from kiosks and *kafenion* also have phones for public use but their charges may be slightly more than the OTE.

For international calls, dial 00, then the country code (44 for the UK; 1 for the US and Canada) followed by the number itself (leaving off the initial zero). AT&T, tel: 00-800-1311; MCI, tel: 00-800-1211.

Calling home

Time

Greece is normally 2 hours ahead of Britain and 7 hours ahead of the US (Eastern Standard Time). Greek summertime – from the last Sunday in March to the last Sunday in September – does not coincide exactly with British summertime, so during certain periods the time difference is 3 hours.

Voltage

220 volts; adaptors (available at any supermarket in Crete) are required for British electrical appliances and transformers for US ones.

Toilets

The toilets in a restaurant may be used without actually buying anything there. There are very few public toilets and those that do exist are not well maintained.

Beaches

In accordance with Greek law, beaches are public places and hotels are not allowed to block admission to their 'strip'.

The beaches are for everyone

Nudism and topless sunbathing

Strictly speaking, nude sunbathing is forbidden except on certain designated beaches. Visitors should respect the sensitivities of the local people, particularly older Greeks, who can be upset by such behaviour, even if they do not show it.

Attitudes are changing towards topless sunbathing and on many beaches in the popular tourist resorts it is now acceptable.

Women Travelling Alone

Women generally encounter few problems when travelling alone, but wearing sensible clothes and keeping on the move will make unwanted approaches less likely. A firm *ochi* (no) is normally sufficient to repel any unwelcome advances. If that does not seem to be having the required effect, then try the Greek term for 'clear off', *fige* (for one) or *figete* (more than one).

Churches are normally closed
if no attendant is present

98

Churches and Monasteries

When entering churches and monasteries, women should cover their shoulders and knees and men ought not to wear shorts. Churches are normally closed if there is no attendant present. Ask at a nearby bar or café if the key is available, but avoid the mid-afternoon siesta period. It is the common practice to thank the keyholder if he has been disturbed by placing a small sum in his hand or leaving a note on the plate by the door.

Photography

Camera film is expensive in Greece so try to buy it in advance. It is normal for photographers to be asked to pay a supplement in museums and the use of tripods is banned, but at archaeological sites there are not usually any restrictions. Photography is not normally permitted in churches.

Radio and Television

ET1 broadcasts the news at 3pm in English, French and German. Most hotels have TV rooms and you'll find virtually all English-language programmes are subtitled rather than dubbed. Many hotels in Greece can now receive satellite TV.

Newspapers

British newspapers usually arrive in Crete a day late. The *Athens News* is an English language daily newspaper.

Medical

The main health hazard in Crete is overexposure to the sun – wear a hat and sunglasses during the summer months and use a high-factor suntan lotion, especially for the first week or so. Also, be sure to drink plenty of fluids to avoid any danger of dehydration.

In cases of illness, attend the nearest hospital or health centre *(kentro ygieias)*. There is one in most of the larger towns. The Greek word for doctor is *iatros* and a dentist is *odontoiatros*. Many Greek doctors studied abroad and usually speak English.

Under EU regulations, British and other EU nationals are entitled to free medical care in Greece (for UK residents to qualify an E111 form must be presented – these are available at any British post office). It should be noted, however, that public health facilities are limited in Greece and private doctors are sometimes the only satisfactory option. Comprehensive travel insurance is a sensible precaution – available from travel agents, banks and insurance brokers, this covers both private medical treatment and loss or theft of personal property.

Pharmacies *(farmakia)* are recognised by a red or green cross on a white background. Greek pharmacists are highly trained and can usually advise on treatments for minor complaints. They are also able to dispense a number of medicines which in other countries are available only on prescription. In the larger towns pharmacists operate a rota to provide 24-hour cover – details are posted in pharmacy windows.

99

Crime

It would not be true to say that Greece is crime-free. Certainly, ten years ago there was very little, but theft is on the increase and visitors should take all the usual precautions that they would at home.

Emergency telephone numbers
Police: tel: 100
Ambulance/first Aid: tel: 166
Fire: tel: 199
Road assistance: tel: 174

Tourist police
Heraklion: tel: (081) 283190
Chania: tel: (0821) 51111 or (0821) 71111
Rethymnon: tel: (0831) 28156
Agios Nikolaos: tel: (0841) 26900

Diplomatic representation
British Embassy: Ploutárchou 1, 106–175 Athens, tel: (01) 723 6211–9; **Consulate**: Papalexándrou 16, Iráklion, tel: (081) 224012
US Embassy: Vassilíssis Sofías 91, 115–121 Athens, tel: (01) 721 2951–9 or (01) 721 8400

Helping out in emergencies

Modern developments

Hotels and private rooms

Most visitors come to Crete on a package tour which includes pre-booked accommodation – this means that during the high season many of the larger resort hotels are fully booked by foreign tour operators. There are, however, good hotels to be found in all the towns. Official tourist offices (EOT, *see page 95*) can also provide a comprehensive list of hotels and pensions.

Hotels are classified into six categories: luxury (L), A, B, C, D and E. Prices are approved by the authorities and are normally shown on a notice in the room. Outside the high season, prices are often considerably cheaper. For this book, the six categories have been reduced to three: L and A (\$\$\$), B and C (\$\$) and D and E (\$).

Rooms in private houses are available in the smallest coastal towns. The quality can vary from the equivalent of B category to just a tiny bedroom. Landlords or their agents often wait for guests at the bus station or by the harbour when a ferry arrives.

100

There are about 20 campsites on Crete and a list of addresses can be obtained from tourist offices. Shady pitches and well-maintained toilet blocks are a rarity, however.

Agia Galini
This beautifully sited resort seems to consist of nothing but hotels and pensions. **\$Candia** is a friendly hotel with a view over the harbour and sea, tel: (0832) 91203 (open all year). The **\$\$Andromeda** pension, tel: (0832) 91284 and **\$\$Rea**, tel: (0832) 91390 are slightly better appointed. **Camp sites: Camping Agia Galini**, reasonable pitches under olives, out of the village on the road to Timbaki.

Agia Pelagia
\$\$Alexander House, good watersport facilities, tel: (081) 811303, fax: 811381. The pretty **\$\$\$Capsis Beach** occupies a whole peninsula, tel: (081) 811212, fax: 811076.

Agia Roumeli
\$\$Agia Roumeli pension only has a few rooms, but they are panelled with wood. Sea view, tel: (0821) 25657.

Agios Georgios
\$Kourites is a basic but good pension in Tzermiado, tel: (0844) 22194. **\$Rea** in Agios Georgios is a more modest establishment but nicely furnished, tel: (0844) 31209.

Agios Nikolaos

Agios Nikolaos
Smaller pensions around the bus station, but **\$\$Alfa** on the peninsula is better, tel: (0841) 23701, and **\$\$Ormos** on

the edge of the town on the Elounda side with bunga-lows and swimming pool, tel: 28144, fax: 25394. If money is no obstacle, then try the luxury **$$$Minos Palace**, built to resemble the architectural style of the Minoan palaces, tel: 23801, fax: 23816.

Almirida
$$Almirida Bay,** 50-bed hotel with restaurant and swim-ming pool, tel: (0821) 31751. **$$Farma Almirida is a pop-ular hotel situated only a few hundred yards from the beach and offers its guests a 'holiday on the farm', tel: (0821) 31732, 31589.

Anogia
$Psiloritis, a small, simple hotel on the main road to Her-aklion, tel: (0834) 31231.

Bali
$$Bali Beach, a single-storey hotel occupying a pleas-ant site on the bay, tel: (0834) 94210. Independent trav-ellers prefer to stay in private rooms and there are plenty to choose from.

Chania
A number of the Venetian town houses have been opu-lently converted into luxurious pensions. Try **$$Casa Delfino**, Theofanous 9, near Zambeliou, tel: (0821) 93098, fax: 96500, or **$$Contessa**, Theofanous 15, with expen-sive furniture, wooden floors and ceilings, tel: 23966. **$$Porto Veneziano** is situated some distance from the bustle of the main harbour near the yacht marina and fish-ing harbour, tel: 59311, fax: 44053. Smaller, quieter beach hotels can be found in Nea Chora, a 15-minute walk from the town centre. **$Elena Beach**, tel: 97633, fax: 92972.

Chania

Chersonisos
Chersonisos has two top-grade luxury hotels. **$$$Creta Maris** by the beach has 1,000 beds, single-storey ac-commodation and a design in sympathy with Cretan ar-chitectural style, tel: (0897) 22115, fax: 22130. **$$$Knossos Royal Village** was opened in 1991 and, as the name suggests, attempts to recreate a Minoan settle-ment, tel: (0897) 23375, fax: 23150. **$Erato** is a quiet, family-run pension in Gouves and can offer good qual-ity accommodation, tel: (081) 761227.

Chora Sfakion
$$Vritomartis, a 100-room hotel just a short distance from the town. Open all year, it is popular with long-stay win-ter guests. Swimming pool and tennis, tel: (0825) 91112, fax: 91222.

Elafonisi

Pensions are being built even at such remote spots as Elafonisi. Try **$Elafonisi Rent Rooms**, tel: (0822) 61123.

Elounda

Of the four luxury hotels **$$$Elounda Beach** (member of the 'Leading Hotels of the World' group, tel: 0841-41812, fax: 41373), and **$$$Elounda Mare** (Relais et Chateaux, tel: 41102, fax: 41307) stand out as the finest. **$$Aristea** is adjacent to the sea, tel: (0841) 41301. **$Olous** on the main street is very reasonable both in price and quality, tel: 41357.

Georgioupolis

Mainly private rooms and pensions. In the east, however, the sandy beach is lined by big hotels. **$Paradise** is a simple pension with clean rooms and good food, in a side road near the *platia*.. **$Zorbas** with 17 rooms has a good reputation, also near the *platia*, tel: (0852) 61381. **$$$Mare Monte** is a pleasant beach hotel with swimming pool and organised activities. Next to the beach, tel: (0852) 61390, fax: 61274.

Heraklion

It is not easy to find a quiet hotel in this noisy town and the beach hotels in the west of the town should be avoided. Light sleepers could ask for a room at the back.
Hotels in the old town: **$Cretan Sun**, tel: (081) 243794. By the market. **$$Daedalus**, tel: 224391. In the pedestrianised zone at the heart of the old town. Relatively quiet. The **$$Lato**, **$$Marin** and the **$$Kris** in the Epimenidou all have a sea view.
Beach hotels: **Agapi Beach**, 6km (4 miles) away by the beach at Ammoudara, tel: (081) 250502, fax: 258371.
Camp sites: The best equipped campsite on Crete – with swimming pool – lies to the west of the town near the village of Ammoudara.

Ierapetra

$$$Lyktos Beach is a beach hotel of superior quality, with tennis courts, 7km (4 miles) out of town, tel: (0842) 61280, fax: 61318. **$Lygia** in a narrow side street off Odhos Ryrba, tel: (0842) 28881 or – not far away – **$Camiros**, tel: 28704.

Kastelli Kissamou

$Galini Beach, pension by the beach, tel: (0822) 23288.

Maleme

$$$Crete Chandris, a pleasant hotel with all the usual facilities. Free bus shuttle to and from Chania, tel: (0821) 62221–4, fax: 62406.

Malia

$$$Hellenic Palace is a modern hotel with 134 rooms. Close to the beach between Malia and Sissi. The much quieter resort of Sissi offers visitors some respite from mass tourism.

Camp sites: Malia Camping is situated – unusually for Crete – in a green location and there is plenty of shade.

Matala

$$Matala Bay is a good hotel, but is some distance from the sea, tel: (0892) 42100. Open all the year round are **$$Eva Maria**, tel: (0892) 42125 and **$$Frangiskos**, tel: (0892) 42380. All three are modern holiday hotels.

Mirtos

$Mirtos,** tel: (0842) 51215. In the middle of the village and open all year. The top address in Mirtos is the modern **$$Esperides with swimming pool, tel: 51207.

Palaeochora

$$Polydoros in a cul-de-sac near the beach. Small but well-appointed, tel: (0823) 41068. **$Hotel Rea** in the town. Twelve clean rooms with bath, tel: (0823) 41307.

Plakias

$Fenix,** to the west of Plakias in a quiet location, tel: (0832) 31331. **$$$Damnoni Resort, a beach hotel with good watersport facilities, tel: (0832) 31991, fax: 31893.

Rethymnon

Small pensions and private rooms near the harbour and between the Arkadiou and the beach. **$$Kyma Beach** on the Platia Iroon, tel: (0831) 55503, fax: 22353. A 35-room hotel with a good *à la carte* menu. It has central heating and stays open all year. A series of A-Category hotels can be found beside the long sandy beach. Try **$$$Grecotel Rethimna Beach**. It offers watersports and children's activities. Mountain bike tours can also be arranged from here, tel: (0831) 21181, fax: 20085.

Sitia

$$$Helios Club, 160-room beach hotel out on the road to Vai, tel: (0841) 28821, fax: 28826. Several C-category hotels with **$$Krystal** the best of the bunch, in the Kapetan Sifi near the harbour, tel: 22284. **$Finikas,** on the edge of town near archaeological museum, tel: (0843) 24955.

Zaros

$$Idi, mountain hotel with an old water mill which still functions. The hotel farms its own trout in a nearby pond. Good restaurant, tel: (0894) 31302.

Sunset on the beach

Rethymnon harbour

Index